PAPAL
WISDOM

WORDS OF HOPE
AND INSPIRATION FROM
JOHN PAUL II

COMPILED BY

Matthew E. Bunson

A DUTTON BOOK

DUTTON
Published by the Penguin Group
Penguin Books USA Inc., 375 Hudson Street,
New York, New York 10014, U.S.A.
Penguin Books Ltd, 27 Wrights Lane,
London W8 5TZ, England
Penguin Books Australia Ltd, Ringwood,
Victoria, Australia
Penguin Books Canada Ltd, 10 Alcorn Avenue,
Toronto, Ontario, Canada M4V 3B2
Penguin Books (N.Z.) Ltd, 182–190 Wairau Road,
Auckland 10, New Zealand

Penguin Books Ltd, Registered Offices:
Harmondsworth, Middlesex, England

First published by Dutton, an imprint of Dutton Signet, a division
of Penguin Books USA, Inc.
Distributed in Canada by McClelland & Stewart Inc.

Excerpts from *Crossing the Threshold of Hope* by His Holiness John Paul II.
Translation Copyright © 1994 by Alfred A. Knopf, Inc. Reprinted by
permission of the publisher.

First Printing, October, 1995
10   9   8   7   6   5   4   3   2   1

REGISTERED TRADEMARK—MARCA REGISTRADA

Library of Congress Cataloging-in-Publication Data

John Paul II, Pope
    Papal wisdom : words of hope and inspiration from John Paul II /
[compiled by] Matthew E. Bunson.
        p.   cm.
    ISBN 0-525-94119-3
    1. Catholic Church—Doctrines—Papal documents.   I. Bunson,
Matthew.   II. Title.
BX1751.2.J6267   1995
282—dc20   95-34978
                                                         CIP
Printed in the United States of America
Set in Berkeley Old Style Book
Designed by Stanley S. Drate/Folio Graphics Co., Inc.

This book is printed on acid-free paper. ♾

ACKNOWLEDGMENTS

There are a number of individuals to whom I would like to express my thanks for their kind assistance in the preparation of this volume. Among them are: Deirdre Mullane; Jacqueline Lindsey and Henry O'Brien; the Daughters of St. Paul; Sarah Davis of the Catholic News Service; the staff of a number of libraries, including the Sahara West Library; Martha Casselman, my exceedingly patient agent; and Danielle Perez of Dutton Signet, the project editor.

CONTENTS

༉

FOREWORD

࿏

> The reverend cardinals have called a new
> Bishop of Rome. The have called him from a
> far country, far but always so close for the com-
> munion in the Christian faith and tradition.

So proclaimed Karol Cardinal Wojtyla, Archbishop of
Cracow on the evening of October 16, 1978, soon
after his election as Pope John Paul II. His elevation
to the papacy, marking the first Polish pope and the
first non-Italian pontiff since 1522, came as a total
surprise to the Church and to the world. It was, however, only the first unexpected event in a reign that
has been the source of frequent happenings and developments unanticipated and unlooked for, earning
the Polish successor to St. Peter the title Pope of Sur-
prises.

Beyond his leadership of the Catholic Church, his
role in the collapse of the Soviet Empire, and his long
efforts at ecumenism and interfaith dialogue, perhaps
John Paul's most surprising achievement has been his
ability to reach beyond the boundaries of the Church

and traditional influence of the Holy See. This pontiff has touched the lives, minds, and hearts of millions, adhering to religions and philosophies of all descriptions, across the globe. He has authored a monumentally bestselling book, *Crossing the Threshold of Hope,* journeyed to nearly every region of the earth, been named *Time* magazine Man of the Year, and amassed a body of philosophical, spiritual, theological, and even poetic writings, translated into hundreds of languages. All of these contribute to making him the best known and most consequential religious figure in modern history, but central to his outreach is the deep spirituality and faith upon which his labors are based.

Determined, vocal, passionate—and some would say controversial—John Paul gives to a world filled with doubts, cynicism, and pervasive uncertainty, moral certitude and solutions to crises that are both contemporary and timeless. He stands as the conscience of our age and, while many may disagree with him, none can ignore him or overlook his impact.

This book offers a collection of the pope's wisdom on a variety of topics, ranging from peace, spirituality, and war, to women, equal justice, and death. While rooted in the Church's tradition and Scripture and its most elevated forms of theology and philosophy—embodied in the classic Scholastic formula of faith and reason—the thoughts, ideas, and prayers of the pope that are presented here nevertheless have a universality of value and application; they are intended for all, Catholic and non-Catholic alike. *Papal Wisdom* is for anyone who shares the pontiff's desire for the advancement of each person's spiritual destiny, their innate dignity, and their equal right to share in the love of God, a fullness of humanity that he has expressed in the complimentary terms of the "culture of life" and the "civilization of love." Above all, the quotations and excerpts seek through their offering of this pope's unannotated, undiluted, and often surprising words, to make manifest John Paul's plea for trust and hope in Christ that began his reign seventeen years ago and which have been echoed since that cool Roman evening in 1978: "Be not afraid!"

PAPAL
WISDOM

❧

CHURCH

Against the spirit of the world, the Church takes up anew each day a struggle that is none other than *the struggle for the world's soul*. If in fact, on the one hand, the Gospel and evangelization are present in this world, on the other, there is also present *a powerful anti-evangelization* which is well-organized and has the means to vigorously oppose the Gospel and evangelization. The struggle for the soul of the contemporary world is at its height where the spirit of this world seems strongest.

Crossing the Threshold of Hope

Being Christians in our day means being builders of communion in the Church and in society.

Slavorum Apostoli, 27

See [the Church] cannot cross the threshold of the new millennium without encouraging her children to purify themselves, through repentance, of past errors and instances of infidelity, inconsistency, and slowness to act. Acknowledging the weaknesses of the past is an act of honesty and courage which helps us to strengthen our faith.

Tertio Millennio Adveniente, 33

ॐ

Holiness . . . must be called a fundamental presupposition and an irreplaceable condition for everyone in fulfilling the mission of salvation within the Church. The Church's holiness is the hidden source and the infallible measure of the works of the apostolate and of the missionary effort. Only in the measure that the Church, Christ's Spouse, is loved by him and she, in turn, loves him, does she become a mother fruitful in the Spirit.

Christifideles Laici, 17

ॐ

I call with all my strength on those who have means and who feel they are Christians, to renew their minds and their hearts in order that, promoting greater justice and even giving something of their own, no one will lack proper food, clothing, housing, culture, and work; all that gives dignity to the human person. The image of Christ on the Cross, the price of the redemption of humanity, is a pressing appeal to spend our lives in putting ourselves at the service of the needy, in harmony with charity, which is generous and which does not sympathize with injustice, but with truth.

Address, Guadalajara, Mexico, 1979

ॐ

The *martyrologium* of the first centuries was the basis of the veneration of the saints. By proclaiming and venerating the holiness of her sons and daughters, the Church gave supreme honor to God himself; in the martyrs she venerated Christ, who was at the origin of their martyrdom and holiness. In later times there developed the practice of canonization, a practice which still continues in the Catholic Church and the Orthodox churches. In recent years the number of canonizations and beatifications has increased. These show the vitality of the local churches, which are much more numerous today than in the first centuries and in the first millennium. The greatest homage which all the churches can give to Christ on the threshold of the third millennium will be to manifest the redeemer's all-powerful presence through the fruits of faith, hope, and charity present in men and women of many different tongues and races who have followed Christ in the various forms of the Christian vocation.

Tertio Millennio Adveniente, 37

ॐ

The Church still has its eschatological awareness. It still leads man to eternal life. If the Church should cease to do so, it would cease being faithful to its vocation, to the New Covenant, which God has made with it in Jesus Christ.

Crossing the Threshold of Hope

᪥

For an adequate participation in ecclesial life the lay faithful absolutely need to have a clear and precise vision of the *particular church with its primordial bond to the Universal Church.* The particular church does not come about from a kind of fragmentation of the universal Church, nor does the universal Church come about by a simple amalgamation of particular churches. Rather, there is a real, essential, and constant bond uniting each of them and this is why the universal Church exists and is manifested in the particular churches.

Christifideles Laici, 25

᪥

Nobody . . . can make of theology as it were a simple collection of his own personal ideas, but everybody must be aware of being in close union with the mission of teaching truth for which the Church is responsible.

Redemptor Hominis, 19

᪥

But how many people have never known . . . joy? They feed on emptiness and tread the paths of despair. "They walk in darkness and the shadow of death" (Lk. 1:79). And we need not look to the far ends of the earth for them. They live in our neighborhoods, they walk down our streets, they may even be members of our own families. They live without true joy because they live without hope. They live without hope because they have never heard, really heard, the Good News of Jesus Christ, because they have never met a brother or a sister who touched their lives with the love of Jesus and lifted them up from their misery.

We must go to them therefore as a messenger of hope. We must bring to them the witness of true joy. We must pledge to them our commitment to work for a just society and city where they feel respected and loved.

Address, New York, 1979

൧

In view of the moral challenges presented by enormous new technological power endangering not only fundamental human rights but the very biological essence of the human species, it is of upmost importance that lay Christians—with the help of the universal Church—take up the task of calling culture back to the principles of an authentic humanism, giving a dynamic and sure foundation to the promotion and defense of the rights of the human being in one's very essence—an essence which the preaching of the Gospel reveals to all.

Christifideles Laici, 38

৵

The Church in our day needs very specially this apostolate of the working class; the apostolate of the workers, and the apostolate among the laboring classes, to enlighten once more with the light of the gospel this important sector of life.

Address, Mayence, 1980

৵

The Church, carrying out her true spiritual mission and always wishing to maintain the greatest respect for the necessary and legitimate institutions of the temporal order, never neglects to appreciate and rejoice in everything that promotes the strength to live the integral truth about man; she cannot neglect to congratulate the efforts that are made to safeguard and defend the rights and fundamental freedom of every human person. She rejoices and thanks the Lord of life and history, when plans and programs—of a political, economic, social, and cultural nature—are inspired by love and respect for the dignity of man, in the search for the "civilization of love."

Address, Rome, 1982

৵

Since the work that awaits everyone in the vineyard of the Lord is so great, there is no place for idleness. With even greater urgency the "householder" repeats his invitation: "you too go into my vineyard."

Christifideles Laici, 3

↭

How then can the Bridegroom's friends fail to remember that he is present, and fail to think back to the days of that birth and death which have shaped their whole lives? Such recollection is more necessary than ever at the present time when attempts are being made to desacralize the whole of human life, to break all its closest ties with Christianity, to sever its link with every human person and with the entire human race through Christ's liberating death and resurrection.

Sign of Contradiction, 11.1

↭

You experience in the Church, in a special way, the dignity of children of God—the noblest, the loveliest title to which a human being can aspire. Keep this dignity alive and operative. In it resides the grandeur that the Church fosters, guards, and promotes. No one has as many reasons to love the poor, respect them, and demand respect for them, as has the Church.

Address, Medellín, Colombia, 1980

↭

The privileged way at present for the creation and transmission of culture is the *means of social communications.* The world of the mass media represents a new frontier for the mission of the Church because it is undergoing a rapid and innovative development and has an extensive worldwide influence on the formation of mentality and customs. In particular, the lay faithful's responsibility as professionals in this field, exercised both by individual right and through community initiatives and institutions, demands that it be sustained by more adequate resource materials, both intellectual and pastoral.

Christifideles Laici, 44

The Church must be present in all areas of human activity, and nothing that is human can remain extraneous to it. And it is principally you, dear lay people, who must make it present. When the Church is accused of being absent from some area, or of not being concerned about some human problem, it would be equivalent to being upset by the absence of wise lay people or of the inactivity of Christians in that specific area of human life. For this reason I address a warm appeal to you: Do not let the Church be absent in any environment of the life of your dear nation. Everything must be permeated by the leaven of the Gospel of Christ and illuminated by its light. It is your duty to do it!

Address, Lisbon, 1982

The path to God is not covered with interior joy alone. Man desires to *bring others* to Him too. He therefore becomes a messenger and apostle of the love of God: "Give thanks to the Lord, acclaim his name; among the nations make known his deeds" (Is. 12:4).

Insegnamenti **V, 3, 1599–1601**

❧

In our own century the martyrs have returned, many of them nameless, *"unknown soldiers"* as it were *of God's great cause.* As far as possible, their witness should not be lost to the Church.

Tertio Millennio Adveniente, **37**

❧

At the end of the second millennium, the Church has once again become a Church of martyrs. The persecution of believers—priests, religious, and laity—has caused a great sowing of martyrdom in different parts of the world. The witness to Christ borne even to the shedding of blood has become a common inheritance of Catholics, Orthodox, Anglicans, and Protestants. . . .

Tertio Millennio Adveniente, **37**

❧

DEATH AND THE AFTERLIFE

In fact, *people of our time have become insensitive to the Last Things* [Death and Judgment, Heaven and Hell]. On the one hand, *secularization and secularism* promote this insensitivity and lead to a consumer mentality oriented toward the enjoyment of earthly goods. On the other hand, the *"hells on earth"* created in this century which is now drawing to a close have also contributed to this insensitivity. After the experience of concentration camps, gulags, bombings, not to mention natural catastrophes, can man possibly expect anything worse from this world, an even greater amount of humiliation and contempt? In a word, hell?

Crossing the Threshold of Hope

"We do not know the time when the earth and humanity will come to an end, and we do not know the way in which the universe will be transformed" (*Gaudium et Spes,* n. 39). But one thing is clear to all of us: our death. "That men die once is certain" (Heb. 9:27). The inevitability of death is known to all alike.

Sign of Contradiction, 18.3

꒰

The last consolation we are seeking together, my dear pilgrims "in the vale of tears" (*Salve Regina),* is the consolation in the face of death. Since our birth we have been going to meet it, but in our old age we become more conscious of its approaching from year to year—if only we do not forcefully suppress it from our thoughts and feelings. The Creator has arranged it so that in old age accepting and standing the test of death is being prepared, made easier and learned in an almost natural manner.

Address, Munich, 1980

꒰

Our modern secularized societies run the risk of driving suffering, dying, and death out of their personal experience.

Ad Limina Address, Rome, 1992

꒰

Revelation progressively allows the first notion of immortal life planted by the Creator in the human heart to be grasped with ever greater clarity: "He has made everything beautiful in its time; also he has put eternity into man's mind" (Eccles. 3:11). This first notion of totality and fullness is waiting to be manifested in love and brought to perfection by God's free gift, through sharing in his eternal life.

Evangelium Vitae, 31

སྲ

So every dying man has in him the biological reality of death, the "dissolution of the body," and also the human experience of dying, in which "the seed of eternity . . . rebels against death," and this seed "is inherent in every man, who cannot be reduced to mere matter"; finally every man has inherent in him the mystery of a new life which Christ has brought and which he has grafted on to humanity.

Jesus, having loved His disciples, loved them to the end. This love is for you too, for you in the first place who belong to the "poor," to those who suffer from limitations in their mind and in their body, but who often understand better than others the need for simple, true relationships, faithful friendship, service freely given, unfailing trust. So enter with Jesus into this charity received and given.

Address, Lourdes, Holy Week, 1981

སྲ

The great school of living and dying, then, brings us to many an open grave; it makes us stand at many a deathbed before it will be us around whom other people will be standing in prayer—so may God grant it.

Address, Munich, 1980

Eternal life is exactly this. The Death of Christ gives life, because it allows believers to share in His Resurrection. The Resurrection is the revelation of life, which is affirmed as present beyond the boundary of death. Before His own Death and Resurrection, Christ raised Lazarus, but before doing so He had a meaningful conversation with Lazarus's sisters. Martha says: "Lord, if you had been here, my brother would not have died." Christ: "Your brother will rise." Martha replies: "I know he will rise, in the resurrection on the last day." And Jesus answers: "I am the resurrection and the life; whoever believes in me, even if he dies, will live, and everyone who lives and believes in me will never die" (Jn. 11:21, 23–26). These words spoken on the occasion of the resurrection of Lazarus contain the truth about the resurrection of the body through Christ. His Resurrection, His victory over death, embraces every man. We are called to salvation, we are called to participate in life, which has been revealed through the Resurrection of Christ.

Crossing the Threshold of Hope

With regard to the last moments of life . . . it would be anachronistic to expect biblical revelation to make express reference to present-day issues concerning respect for elderly and sick persons, or to condemn explicitly attempts to hasten their end by force. The cultural and religious context of the Bible is in no way touched by such temptations; indeed, in that context the wisdom and experience of the elderly are recognized as a unique source of enrichment for the family and for society.

Evangelium Vitae, **46**

꙳

Part of the law of suffering—a law which is, however, less inflexible than that of death—is that it entails loneliness for man. The loneliness is not always evident, nor does it occur at every level of suffering. The limits of human endurance are not reached in every illness; but the closer the suffering gets to those limits, the more the sufferer has to endure it alone. That loneliness can be seen in the story of the just man Job. And when loneliness becomes the occasion for man to meet God, the purifying dimension of suffering is seen to extend beyond the confines of this life.

Sign of Contradiction, **19.3**

꙳

The certainty of future immortality and hope in the promised resurrection cast new light on the mystery of suffering and death, and fill the believer with an extraordinary capacity to trust fully in the plan of God.

Evangelium Vitae, 67

☙

Man heard for the first time the words "you shall die," without having any familiarity with them in his experience up to then. But on the other hand, he could not but associate the meaning of death with that dimension of life which he had enjoyed up to then. The words of God-Yahweh addressed to man confirmed a dependence in existing, such as to make man a limited being and, by his very nature, liable to nonexistence.

Address, Rome, 1979

☙

In *Christianity time has a fundamental importance.* Within the dimension of time the world was created; within it the history of salvation unfolds, finding its culmination in the "fullness of time" of the Incarnation and its goal in the glorious return of the Son of God at the end of time. . . . With the coming of Christ there begin "the last days" (cf. Heb. 1:2), the "last hour" (cf. 1 Jn. 2:18), and the time of the Church which will last until the Parousia [the return of Christ].

Tertio Millennio Adveniente, 10

☙

Human life and death are thus in the hands of God, in his power: "In his hand is the life of every living thing and the breath of all mankind," exclaims Job (12:10). "The Lord brings to death and brings to life; he brings down to Sheol and raises up" (1 Sm. 2:6). He alone can say: "It is I who bring both death and life" (Dt. 32:39). But God does not exercise this power in an arbitrary and threatening way, but rather as part of his care and loving concern for his creatures. If it is true that human life is in the hands of God, it is no less true that these are loving hands, like those of a mother who accepts, nurtures, and takes care of her child: "I have calmed and quieted my soul like a child quieted at its mother's breast; like a child that is quieted is my soul" (Ps. 131:2; cf. Is. 49:15; 66:12–13; Hos. 11:4). Thus Israel does not see in the history of peoples and in the destiny of individuals the outcome of mere chance or of blind fate, but rather the results of a loving plan by which God brings together all the possibilities of life and opposes the powers of death arising from sin: "God did not make death, and he does not delight in the death of the living. For he created all things that they might exist" (Wis. 1:13–14).

Evangelium Vitae, 39

⁂

The Church *prays for the dead* and this prayer says much about the reality of the Church itself. It says that the Church continues to live in the *hope of eternal life*. Prayer for the dead and destruction that weighs down upon the earthly existence of man. This is and remains a particular *revelation of the Resurrection*. In this prayer Christ Himself bears witness to the life and immortality, to which God calls every human being.

Crossing the Threshold of Hope

༄

The request which arises from the human heart in the supreme confrontation with suffering and death, especially when faced with the temptation to give up in utter desperation, is above all a request for companionship, sympathy, and support in the time of trial. It is a plea for help to keep on hoping when all human hopes fail.

Evangelium Vitae, 67

༄

Without familiarity with God there is in the last end no consolation in death. For that is exactly what God intends with death, that at least in this one sublime hour of our life we allow ourselves to fall into His love without any other security than just this love of His. How could we show Him our faith, our hope, our love in a more lucid manner!

One last consideration in this context. I am sure it echoes the conviction of many a heart. Death itself is a consolation! Life on this earth, even if it were no "vale of tears," could not offer a home to us forever. It would turn more and more into a prison, an "exile" (*Salve Regina*). "For all that passes is just a parable!" (Goethe, *Faust* II, final chorus). And so the words of St. Augustine, which never lose their color, come to our lips: "You have created us for Yourself, Lord; and our heart is restless until it finds its rest in You!" (*Confessiones* I, 1, 1.)

Address, Munich, 1980

✌

FAMILY

The family is the center and the heart of the civilization of love.

Letter to Families, 13

⚮

You families that can enjoy prosperity, do not shut yourselves up in your happiness; open up to others to distribute what is superfluous for you and what others lack. Families oppressed by poverty, do not lose heart, and, without taking luxury as your ideal, or riches as the principle of happiness, seek with the help of all to overcome difficult moments while waiting for better days. Families visited and tormented by physical or moral pain, sorely tried by sickness or want, do not add to these sufferings bitterness or despair, but temper sorrow with hope.

Homily, Puebla, Mexico, 1979

⚮

Marriage and the family are very deeply connected with man's personal dignity. They are not derived only from instinct and passion, nor only from feeling; they are derived in the first place from a decision of the free will, from a personal love, because of which spouses become not only one flesh, but also one heart and soul.

Address, Cologne, Germany, 1980

ॐ

The union of hearts! There are innumerable fine shades of difference between the love of man and that of woman. Neither of the partners can demand to be loved in the same way as he or she loves. It is important—on both sides—to renounce the secret reproaches that separate hearts and to free oneself of this sorrow at the most favorite moment. *To share the joys and, even more so, the sufferings of the heart, is a strong bond of unity. But it is just as much in common love of the children that the union of hearts is strengthened.*

Homily, Kinshasa, Zaire, 1980

ॐ

During recent decades many families . . . remained the true sanctuaries of faith, love, and fidelity to Christ and the Church. The dangers that threaten its integrity today are strong. The new evangelization must give priority to the spiritual needs of the family. The holiness and indissolubility of marriage must be proclaimed with all your might, as the cause of the mutual perfection of husband and wife and of their intimate human wealth, and as a prerequisite for safe-guarding the sacrosanct values of the nation. Nascent life must be protected from the first instant of conception, and you must continue to educate the young generations so that they may discover the true meaning of love and responsible parenthood.

Ad Limina **Address, 1992**

ॐ

Man is not meant to be alone. He does not exist alone on earth. He is called to live his life in community. For this reason communities are born, the first and most fundamental of which is precisely the family. And by means of communities, the first of which is the family, man is formed and matures as man. So, born into the marriage community of man and woman, man owes his education to the family. Education, in keeping with the special meaning of this word, is intended to "humanize" man. Man, from the first moment of his conception in his mother's womb, gradually learns to be a man: and this fundamental training period is identified precisely with education. Man is the future of the family itself and of all mankind, but his future is inseparably bound to education.

Address, Lisbon, 1982

ॐ

It is in the family, I believe, that we find a human resource which produces the best creative energies of the social fabric. This is something which every state ought carefully to safeguard. Without infringing on the autonomy of a reality which they can neither produce nor replace, civil authorities have a duty, in effect, to strive to promote the harmonious growth of the family, not only from the point of view of its social vitality but also from that of its moral and spiritual health.

Papal Letter to Leaders of the World, 1994

჻

Knowing that marriage and the family constitute one of the most precious of human values, the Church wishes to speak and offer her help to those who are already aware of the value of marriage and the family and seek to live it faithfully, to those who are uncertain and anxious and searching for the truth, and to those who are unjustly impeded from living freely their family lives. Supporting the first, illuminating the second, and assisting the others, the Church offers her services to every person who wonders about the destiny of marriage and the family.

Familiaris Consortio, 1

჻

Television can enrich family life. It can draw family members closer together and foster their solidarity with other families and with the community at large. It can increase not only their general knowledge but also their religious knowledge, making it possible for them to hear God's word, to strengthen their religious identity, and to nurture their moral and spiritual life. . . . Television can also harm family life: by propagating degrading values and models of behavior, by broadcasting pornography and graphic depictions of brutal violence; by inculcating oral relativism and religious skepticism; by spreading distorted, manipulative accounts of news events and current issues; by carrying exploitative advertising that appeals to base instincts, and by glorifying false visions of mutual respect, of justice and of peace.

Message for World Communications Day, 1994

ン

In affirming that the spouses, as parents, cooperate with God the Creator in conceiving and giving birth to a new human being, we are not speaking merely with reference to the laws of biology. Instead, we wish to emphasize that God *himself is present in human fatherhood and motherhood* quite differently than he is present in all other instances of begetting "on earth." Indeed, God alone is the source of that "image and likeness" which is proper to the human being, as it was received at Creation. Begetting is the continuation of creation.

Letter to Families, 9

↭

The great danger for family life in the midst of any society whose idols are pleasure, comfort, and independence, lies in the fact that people close their hearts and become selfish. *The fear of making permanent commitments can change the mutual love of husband and wife into two loves of self,* two loves existing side by side until they end in separation.

Homily, Washington, D. C., 1979

↭

Tomorrow's adults are the children of today. To overlook this elementary fact not only compromises the future of the child, but that of society as such.

Address, Rome, 1993

↭

When a new person is born of the conjugal union of the two, he brings with him into the world a particular image and likeness of God himself: The genealogy of the person is inscribed in the very biology of generation. In affirming that the spouses, as parents, cooperate with God the Creator in conceiving and giving birth to a new human being, we are not speaking merely with reference to the laws of biology. Instead, we wish to emphasize that God himself is present in human fatherhood and motherhood quite differently than he is present in all other instances of begetting "on earth." Indeed, God alone is the source of that "image and likeness" which is proper to the human being, as it was received at creation. Begetting is the continuing of creation.

Evangelium Vitae, 43

ॐ

An institution as natural, universal, and fundamental as the family cannot be manipulated without causing serious damage to the fabric and stability of society.

Message to the UN Population Fund Director, 1994

ॐ

. . . Ideologies and various systems, together with forms of uninterest and indifference, dare to take over the role in education proper to the family. . . . Required in the face of this is a vast, extensive, and systematic work, sustained not only by culture but also by economic and legislative means, which will safeguard the role of family in its task of being the *primary place of "humanization"* for the person and society.

Christifideles Laici, 40

ॐ

Motherhood is the fruit of the marriage union of a man and woman, of that biblical "knowledge" which corresponds to the "union of the two in one flesh" (cf. Gen. 2:24). This brings about—on the woman's part—a special "gift of self," as an expression of that spousal love whereby the two are united to each other so closely that they become "one flesh". . . . This *mutual gift of the person in marriage* opens to the gift of a new life, *a new human being,* who is also a person in the likeness of his parents.

Mulieris Dignitatem, 18

༈

Conscious of their own rights, families will be able to make their voices heard with greater authority in the forums where laws and policies concerning the family are formulated.

Address, Rome, 1993

༈

The family must go back to the "beginning" of God's creative act, if it is to attain self-knowledge and self-realization in accordance with the inner truth not only of what it is but also of what it does in history. And since in God's plan it has been established as an "intimate community of life and love," the family has the mission to become more and more what it is, that is to say, a community of life and love. . . . Looking at it in such a way as to reach its very roots, we must say that the essence and role of the family are in the final analysis specified by love.

Familiaris Consortio, 17

જી

The family is the basic cell of society. It is the cradle of life and love, the place in which the individual "is born" and "grows."

Christifideles Laici, 40

જી

Mankind's future rests in, and depends upon, the family, more than any other society, institution, or environment. This truth rang out in Abram's conversation with God heard moments ago in the reading of the expressive page from Genesis: "Your reward shall be very great," the Lord promised to His friend. "What will you give me, Lord?" Abram asked with a shade of skepticism, "for I continue childless . . ." (cf. Gen. 15:2). Abram's dejected prostration will be followed by his joy when, "at the time of which God had spoken to him" (Gen. 21:2) Sarah will give him a son. Mankind's future is, first of all, man himself. It is man born from man: from a father and a mother, from a man and a woman. For this reason, mankind's future is determined in the family.

Homily, Mt. Samiero, Portugal, 1982

જી

The eternal mystery of generation, which is in God himself, the one and Triune God (cf. Eph. 3:14–15), is reflected in the woman's motherhood and in the man's fatherhood. Human parenthood is something shared by both the man and the woman. Even if the woman, out of love for her husband, says: "I have given you a child," her words also mean: "This is our child."

Mulieris Dignitatem, 14

⌇

The rights of the child may be summarized in its right to be loved, and the community cannot pretend to defend, protect, and support the child's development, if its initiatives are not based on a renewed awareness of the duty to love the child.

Address, Rome, 1993

⌇

Marriage is a unique communion of persons, and it is on the basis of this communion that the family is called to become a community of persons. This is a commitment which the bride and groom undertake "before God and his Church," as the celebrant reminds them before they exchange their consent. . . . The good of both, which is at the same time the good of each, must then become the good of children. The common good, by its very nature, both unites individual persons and ensures the true good of each.

Letter to Families, 10

୬

It is just to the oldest that we must look with respect ("honor!"); to them, families owe their existence, education, and maintenance, which have often been paid for with hard work and much suffering.

General Audience, Rome, 1978

୬

No human society can run the risk of permissiveness in fundamental issues regarding the nature of marriage and the family! Such moral permissiveness cannot fail to damage the authentic requirements of peace and communion among people. It is thus quite understandable why the Church vigorously defends the identity of the family and encourages responsible individuals and institutions, especially political leaders and international organizations, not to yield to the temptation of a superficial and false modernity.

Letter to Families, 17

୬

. . . A person normally comes into the world within a family, and can be said to owe to the family the very fact of his existing as an individual. When he has no family, the person coming into the world develops an anguished sense of pain and loss, one which will subsequently burden his whole life. The Church draws near with loving concern to all who experience situations such as these, for she knows well the fundamental role which the family is called upon to play. Furthermore, she knows that a person goes forth from the family in order to realize in a new family unit his particular vocation in life. Even if someone chooses to remain single, the family continues to be, as it were, his existential horizon, that fundamental community in which the whole network of social relations is grounded, from the closest and most immediate to the most distant. Do we not often speak of the "human family" when referring to all the people living in the world?

Letter to Families, 2

☙

The physical and at the same time spiritual nature of conjugal communion, always enlightened by personal love, must lead to respect for sexuality, its fully human dimension, and never to use it as an "object," in order not to dissolve the personal union of soul and body. . . . The responsibility for the generation of human life—the life which must be born in a family—is great before God!

Address, Lisbon, 1982

☙

When a man and a woman in marriage mutually give and receive each other in the unity of "one flesh," the logic of the sincere gift of self becomes a part of their life. Without this, marriage would be empty; whereas a communion of persons, built on this logic, becomes a communion of parents. When they transmit *life to the child, a new human "thou" becomes a part of the horizon of the "we" of the spouses,* a person whom they will call by a new name: "our son . . . ; our daughter . . ." The newborn child gives itself to its parents by the very fact of its coming into existence. *Its existence is already a gift, the first gift of the Creator to the creature.*

Letter to Families, 11

⤳

There are cultures which manifest a unique veneration and great love for the elderly: far from being outcasts from the family or merely tolerated as a useless burden, they continue to be present and to take an active and responsible part in family life, though having to respect the autonomy of the new family; above all they carry out the important mission of being a witness to the past and a source of wisdom for the young and for the future.

"The Role of the Christian Family in the Modern World," 27

⤳

The ministry of evangelization carried out by Christian parents is original and irreplaceable. It assumes the characteristics typical of family life itself, which should be interwoven with love, simplicity, practicality, and daily witness.

Familiaris Consortio, 53

✥

The rights of the family are closely *linked to the rights of the person:* if in fact the family is a communion of persons, its self-realization will depend in large part on the correct application of the rights of its members.

Letter to Families, 17

✥

The reciprocal co-penetration of divine love and human love lasts from the day of your marriage. Divine love, in fact, penetrates into human love, giving it a new dimension: it makes it deep, pure, and generous; *it develops it toward fullness, ennobles it, spiritualizes it, makes it ready even for sacrifices and self-denial, and at the same time enables it to produce peace and joy as its fruit.*

Address, Rome, 1981

✥

The family is a community of persons and the smallest social unit. As such it is an *institution* fundamental to the life of every society.

Letter to Families, 17

✥

As experience testifies, whole civilizations and the cohesiveness of peoples depend above all on the human quality of their families. For this reason the duty in the apostolate towards family acquires an incomparable social value.

Christifideles Laici, **40**

༈

The family has always been considered as the first and basic expression of man's *social nature.* Even today this way of looking at things remains unchanged. Nowadays, however, emphasis tends to be laid on how much the family, as the smallest and most basic human community, owes to the personal contribution of a man and a woman. The family is in fact a community of persons whose proper way of existing and living together is communion: *communio personarum.* Here, too, while always acknowledging the absolute transcendence of the Creator with regard to his creatures, we can see the family's ultimate relationship to the divine "We." *Only persons are capable of living "in communion."*

Letter to Families, **7**

༈

Families should be the first to take steps to see that the laws and institutions of the State not only do not offend but support and positively defend the rights and duties of the family . . . otherwise families will be the first victims of the evils that they have done no more than note with indifference.

Familiaris Consortio, 24

༄

In the newborn child is realized the common good of the family. Just as the common good of spouses is fulfilled in conjugal love, ever ready to give and receive life, so too the common good of the family is fulfilled through that same spousal love, as embodied in the newborn child. Part of the genealogy of the person is the genealogy of the family, preserved for posterity by the annotations in the Church's baptismal registers, even though these are merely the social consequences of the fact that "a man has been born into the world" (cf. Jn. 16:21).

Letter to Families, 11

༄

*T*he old . . . are extremely precious, and I would say indispensable, for the family and for society. How much help they are to young parents and their children with their knowledge and experience! Their advice and their action also benefit so many groups, in which they, too, have their places, and so many initiatives in the sphere of ecclesial and civil life. Let us all be grateful for this!

Address, Rome, 1982

༄

HUMANITY

Man is called to a fullness of life which far exceeds the dimensions of his earthly existence because it consists in sharing the very life of God. The loftiness of this supernatural vocation reveals the greatness and the inestimable value of human life even in its temporal phase. Life in time, in fact, is the fundamental condition, the initial stage and integral part of the entire unified process of human existence. It is a process which, unexpectedly and undeservedly, is enlightened by the promise and renewed by the gift of divine life, which will reach its full realization in eternity.

Evangelium Vitae, 2

Man who, in his reality has, because he is a "person," a history of his life that is his own and, most important, a history of his soul that is his own. Man who, in keeping with the openness of his spirit within and also with the many diverse needs of his body and his existence in time, writes this personal history of his through numerous bonds, contacts, situations, and social structures linking him with other men, beginning to do so from the first moment of his existence on earth, from the moment of his conception and birth. Man in the full truth of his existence, of his personal being and also of his community and social being—in the sphere of his own family, in the sphere of society and very diverse contexts, in the sphere of his own nation or people (perhaps still only that of his clan or tribe), and in the sphere of the whole of mankind.

Redemptor Hominis, 14

↬

The integral development of the human person through work does not impede but rather promotes the greater productivity and efficiency of work itself, even though it may weaken consolidated power structures. A business cannot be considered only as a "society of capital goods"; it is also a "society of persons" in which people participate in different ways and with specific responsibilities, whether they supply the necessary capital for the company's activities or take part in such activities through their labor. To achieve these goals there is still need for a broad associated workers' movement, directed towards the liberation and promotion of the whole person.

Centessimus Annus, 43

↬

Man must work out of regard for others, especially his own family, but also for the society he belongs to, the country of which he is a child, and the whole human family of which he is a member, since he is the heir to the work of generations and at the same time a sharer in building the future of those who will come after him in the succession of history. All this constitutes the moral obligation of work, understood in its wide sense.

Laborem Exercens, **16**

ॐ

I do not hesitate to proclaim before you and before the world that *all human life—from the moment of conception and through all subsequent stages—is sacred, because human life is created in the image and likeness of God. Nothing surpasses the greatness or dignity of a human person. Human life is not just an idea or an abstraction; human life is the concrete reality of a being that lives, that acts, that grows and develops; human life is the concrete reality of a being that is capable of love, and of service to humanity.*

Homily, Washington, D. C., 1979

ॐ

And in all this—love,
which springs from freedom,
as water springs from an oblique rift in the earth.
This is man! He is not transparent,
not monumental,

not simple,
in fact he is poor.
This is one man—and what about two people, four,
a hundred,
a million—
multiply all this
(multiply the greatness by the weakness),
and you will have the product of humanity,
the product of human life.

The Jeweler's Shop, Act II

ॐ

The fact that man is made "in the image and likeness of God" means, among other things, that he is capable of receiving God's gift; that he is aware of this gift, and that he can respond to it. Precisely for this reason God, from the beginning, established an alliance with man, and with man alone. The book of Genesis reveals to us not only the natural order of existence, but at the same time, and from the beginning, the supernatural order of grace. We can speak of grace only if we admit the reality of God's gift.

Audience, Rome, December 1978

ॐ

Man lives at the same time both in the world of material values and in that of spiritual values. For the individual living and hoping man, his needs, freedoms, and relationship with others never concern one sphere of values alone, but belong to both. Material and spiritual realities may be viewed separately in order to understand better that in the concrete human being they are inseparable, and to see that any threat to human rights, whether in the field of material realities or in that of spiritual realities, is equally dangerous for peace, since in every instance it concerns man in his entirety. Permit me, distinguished ladies and gentlemen, to recall a constant rule of the history of humanity, a rule that is implicitly contained in all that I have already stated with regard to integral development and human rights. The rule is based on the relationship between spiritual values and material or economic values. In this relationship, it is the spiritual values that are preeminent, both on account of the nature of these values and also for reasons concerning the good of man. The preeminence of the values of the spirit defines the proper sense of earthly material goods and the way to use them. This preeminence is therefore at the basis of just peace. It is also a contributing factor to ensuring that material development, technical development, and the development of civilization are at the service of what constitutes man.

Address to the UN, October 1979

ॐ

There does not exist any other possibility of eliminating the consequences of those errors except the patient construction of the foundation of a just system of work which overcomes in its very basis the opposition between labor and capital, through an effort at being shaped in accordance with the principle . . . of the substantial and real priority of labor, of the subjectivity of human labor, and its effective participation in the whole production process.

Laborem Exercens, 13

ॐ

Hands are the heart's landscape. They split sometimes like ravines into which an undefined force rolls.
The very same hands that a man only opens
when his palms have had their fill of toil.
Now he sees: because of him others walk in peace.

from "The Quarry"

ॐ

In our time, *the role of human work* is becoming increasingly important as the productive factor both of nonmaterial and of material wealth. Moreover, it is becoming clearer how a person's work is naturally interrelated with the work of others. More than ever, work is *work with others* and *work for others:* it is a matter of doing something for someone else. Work becomes ever more fruitful and productive to the extent that people become more knowledgeable of the productive potentialities of the earth and more profoundly cognizant of the needs of those for whom their work is done.

Centessimus Annus, 31

༄

Human suffering is a continent of which none of us can claim to have reached the boundaries. But walking through the wards of this "Little House," one explores it in such a way that is more than sufficient to have an idea of its impressive proportions. And the question presents itself: Why?

Address, Rome, 1980

༄

Is it possible to philosophize about what is "substantially human" without referring to the complete experience of man? Who has a right to affirm that this full experience of man is to be found in the slogan "Seek nothing above thyself"? Who has the right to affirm that the full development of man is attained by what closes that experience, and not, instead, by its opening out onto that "Seek beyond thyself"?

Audience, Rome, 1979

༄

Brothers and sisters of the older generation, you are a treasure for the Church, you are a blessing for the world! How often you have to relieve the young parents, how well you know how to introduce the youngsters to the history of your family and your home country, to the tales of your people and to the world of faith! The young adults with their problems often find an easier way to you than to their parents' generation. To your sons and daughters you are the most precious support in their hours of difficulty. With your advice and your engagement you cooperate in many committees, associations, and initiatives of ecclesiastical and public life.

Address, Munich, Germany, 1980

꒰

All of humanity must think of the parable of the rich man and the beggar. Humanity must translate it into contemporary terms, in terms of economy and politics, in terms of all human rights, in terms of relations between the "First," "Second," and "Third World." We cannot stand idly by when thousands of human beings are dying of hunger. Nor can we remain indifferent when the rights of the human spirit are tramped upon, when violence is done to the human conscience in matters of truth, religion, and cultural creativity.

Address to Journalists, 1979

꒰

We are the people of life because God, in his unconditional love, has given us the Gospel of life and by this same Gospel we have been transformed and saved. We have been sent. For us, being at the service of life is not a boast but rather a duty, born of our own awareness of being "God's own people, that we may declare the wonderful deeds of him who called us out of darkness into his marvelous light."

Evangelium Vitae, **93**

꒰

[M]an is a] pilgrim all his life, a pilgrim of the Absolute, traveling towards a goal, seeking the face of God.

Audience, Rome, 1986

꒰

The Pope bows with devotion before old age, and he invites all people to do the same with him. Old age is the crown of the steps of life. It gathers in the harvest, the harvest from what you have learned and experienced, the harvest from what you have done and achieved, the harvest from what you have suffered and undergone. As in the finale of a great symphony, all the great themes of life combine to a mighty harmony.

Address, Munich, 1980

꒰

It is important that the greater awareness and sensitivity now existing should be embodied in appropriate legislation and that those who are active in the fields of medicine, psychology, sociology, and education should foster the full integration of the handicapped person into society. But it is no less important that there should be a change of heart, a conversion, on the part of every citizen and every group in society, so that they may willingly and fraternally accept the presence of handicapped persons at school, at work, and in every activity, including sports.

**Address, Second International Games
for the Disabled, Rome, 1981**

ઝ

In the biblical narrative, the difference between man and other creatures is shown above all by the fact that only the creation of man is presented as the result of a special decision on the part of God, a deliberation to establish a particular and specific bond with the Creator: "Let us make man in our image, after our likeness" (Gn. 1:26). The life which God offers to man is a gift by which God shares something of himself with his creature.

Evangelium Vitae, 34

ઝ

From the most remote times God is represented to us as the "Maker," as the One who does things; and he has entrusted his own work as a heritage to man. So that he might take care of it and use it for his own life and development. Man's creative familiarity with the work of creation finds its expression in all forms of work, material or intellectual, in the work of the artisan, in industry, in service enterprises, and in cultural activities. Work . . . manifests man's resemblance to God, and by so doing constitutes the indispensable foundation of human dignity. The Son of God himself became man in a family of working people; he learned to be an artisan, and called as his disciples men belonging to the working class.

Address, Rome, 1987

જી

Life is the time that is granted to us to express concretely the potential riches which each of us bears and to make our contribution to the common progress of mankind. Life is the time that is given to us to embody in ourselves and in history the values of love, goodness, joy, justice, and peace, to which the human heart aspires.

Address, Rome, 1981

જી

. . . Humankind, created for freedom, bears within itself the wound of original sin, which constantly draws persons toward evil and puts them in need of redemption. Not only is *this doctrine an integral part of Christian revelation;* it also has great hermeneutical value insofar as it helps one to understand human reality. The human person tends toward good, but is also capable of evil. One can transcend one's immediate interest and still remain bound to it. The social order will be all the more stable, the more it takes this fact into account and does not place in opposition personal interest and the interests of society as a whole, but rather seeks ways to bring them into fruitful harmony. In fact, where self-interest is violently suppressed, it is replaced by a burdensome system of bureaucratic control which dries up the wellspring of initiative and creativity.

Centessimus Annus, 25

And you, who are you? For me you are first and foremost human persons, rich in the immense dignity which the state of persons gives you, rich, each one, in the personal, unique and unrepeatable character with which God made you. You are persons redeemed by the blood of Him whom I like to call, as I did in my first letter written to the whole Church and to the world, the "Redeemer of man."

Address, Belém, Brazil, 1980

In the unfailing and necessary reflection that man, in any age, is impelled to make about his own life, two questions come strongly to the fore, an echo as it were of God's voice: "Where do we come from? Where are we going?"

Audience, Rome, 1986

The human conscience does not only accuse man and subject him to gnawing remorse; it also commends and praises him, and "love rejoices in the truth" (1 Cor. 13:6). In man's estimation the silent but positive approval given him by his own quiet conscience far outweighs the most appalling suffering. We can think of men who even under torture have refused to betray their own conscience; we can think of the first Christians who refused to deny Christ because Christ had become their conscience. Even in human society at large there is this tendency to applaud any noble and worthy act; although the tendency here is less than steady, threatened as it is at every turn by subjectivism of all kinds and by a utilitarian outlook on life. But even history rejoices when it can manifest the true glory of man.

Sign of Contradiction, 20.4

꙳

The shape of the face says everything
(where else such expression of being?).
How telling the eyes of a child,
constantly crossing a strange equator
(the earth remains a small atom of thought).

And who is to come?

Everything else enclosed in itself:
grass on the crest of the wind,

an apple tree cradled in space
abundant with fruit.
Man meets Him who walks always ahead,
courage their meeting place,
each man a fortress.

**"A Bishop's Thoughts on Giving the Sacrament of Confirmation
in a Mountain Village"**

ぷ

Despite all the powerful forces of poverty and oppression, of evil and sin in all their forms, *the power
of truth will prevail*—the truth about God, *the truth
about man.*

Address, Delhi, 1986

ぷ

It is also a marvelous challenge for all the peoples
and nations of the world—now that every day we become more aware of our interdependence—to be
called upon by the urgent demands of a new solidarity that knows no frontiers. Now that we move
toward the threshold of the third millennium of
Christianity, we are given the unique chance, for the
first time in human history, *to make a decisive contribution to the building up of a true world community.* The
awareness that we are linked in common destiny is
becoming stronger; the efforts to reach that goal are
being multiplied by men and women of good will in
a diversity of activities—political as well as economic,
cultural as well as social. People in all wakes of life

and nations and governments alike are being challenged in the name of our common humanity, in the name of the rights of every human being and in the name of the rights of every nation.

Address, Detroit, 1987

ॐ

Labor is . . . the fundamental dimension of human earthly existence. It has not only technical but also ethical significance for man. Man is "master" of the earth only as much as he is a master and not a slave of labor. Labor should help man become better, spiritually more mature, more responsible, help him to fulfill his human calling both as an individual and as a member of a community, and above all, as a member of the basic human community, the family.

Address to Workers, Czestochowa, Poland, 1979

ॐ

Only man is capable of work, and only man works, at the same time by work occupying his existence on earth. Thus work bears a particular mark of man and of humanity, the mark of a person operating within a community of persons. And this mark decides its interior characteristics; in a sense it constitutes its very nature.

Laborem Exercens, **Preface**

ॐ

While it is true that man eats the bread produced by the work of his hands—and this means not only the daily bread by which his body keeps alive but also the bread of science and progress, civilization and culture—it is also a perennial truth that he eats this bread by *"the sweat of his face,"* that is to say, not only by personal effort and toil but also in the midst of many tensions, conflicts, and crises, which, in relationship with the reality of work, disturb the life of individual societies and also of all humanity.

Laborem Exercens, 1

❧

This is the meaning of suffering, which is truly supernatural, and at the same time, human. It is supernatural because it is rooted in the divine mystery of the Redemption of the world, and it is likewise deeply human because in it, the person discovers himself, his own humanity, his own dignity, his own mission.

Salvifici Doloris, 2

❧

The truth which we owe to humanity is above all a truth concerning humanity itself. As witnesses of Jesus Christ we are heralds, mouthpieces, servants of that truth which we cannot reduce to the principles of a philosophical system, or to a mere political activity. We cannot forget it, or betray it.

Insegnamenti II, 219–220

❧

Even if machines have improved the living conditions of the workers, after the first impact of novelty it became clear that mechanical precision and speed, greater every day, had begun a new condition of human life. It is the machine that imposes its rhythm upon man; there is no longer time for anything, nor for anyone, with all the problems that arise from this.

However, it should not be like that. Even when it is meant to improve his standard of living, to subject man, "created in the image of God," to a productive effort, directed almost entirely towards material well-being and profit, shutting him off from the prospects of the human and spiritual order, it opposes his dignity.

Address, Porto, Portugal, 1982

৵

I do not hesitate to proclaim before you and before the world that all human life—from the moment of conception through all subsequent stages—is sacred because human life is created in the image and likeness of God. Nothing surpasses the greatness or dignity of a human person.

Address, Washington, DC, 1979

৵

I am firmly convinced that this dialogue between the Church and culture is of great importance for the future of mankind. There are two main and complementary aspects of the question that correspond to the two dimensions in which the Church acts. One is the dimension of the evangelization of cultures and the other is of the defense of man and his cultural advancement.

Address, Korea, 1984

࿘

If work is for man and not man for work, the gradual solution of the problems of the working world must be sought in the effort to create a conscience that is more just, more Christian, and more human.

Address, Porto, Portugal, 1982

࿘

Human life is not just an idea or an abstraction; human life is the concrete reality of a being that lives, that acts, that grows and develops; human life is the concrete reality of a being that is capable of love, and of service to humanity.

Address, Washington, DC, 1979

࿘

. . . Call upon men to open to Jesus Christ, in Him will they learn again their essential dignity as children of God, made in God's image, endowed with unsuspected possibilities which make them capable of facing up to the tasks of the hour, bound to one another by a brotherhood which has its roots in God's father-hood.

"Development in Freedom," 1978

༈

The primacy given to the call of every Christian to holiness, as it is manifested "in the fruits of grace which the spirit produces in the faithful" and in a growth toward the fullness of Christian life and the perfection of charity.

Christifideles Laici, 30

༈

Today more than ever, many persons are tormented by the problem of existence and their own identity. They feel the longing to go beyond the limits of history and time, they feverishly look for truth!

Audience, Rome, 1980

༈

As is plain, the necessity which . . . Christ lays on all His actual and potential listeners, belongs to the interior space in which man—precisely the one who is listening to Him—must perceive anew the lost fullness of his humanity, and want to regain it. . . . Human life, by its nature, is "coeducative" and its dignity, its balance, depends, at every moment in history and at every point of geographical longitude and latitude, on "who" she will be for him and he for her.

Audience, Rome, 1980

જૂ

Man . . . belongs to the visible world; he is a body among bodies. Taking up again and, in a way, reconstructing the meaning of original solitude, we apply it to man in his totality. His body, through which man participates in the visible created world, makes him at the same time conscious of being "alone."

Address, Rome, 1979

જૂ

Always remember that pain is never fruitless, never useless. In fact, at the very moment it wounds your existence, limiting it in its human performance, if it is raised to a supernatural dimension, it can exalt and redeem this existence for a superior destiny, which goes beyond the threshold of the personal situation to reach the whole of society, in such need of those who are able to suffer and offer themselves for its redemption.

Address, Salvador da Bahia, 1980

જૂ

Different languages have different words to express what no one would ever wish to lose under any circumstances, what constitutes the expectation, longing and hope of all mankind. But there is no better word than "life" to sum up comprehensively the greatest aspiration of all humanity. "Life" indicates the sum total of all the goods that people desire, and at the same time what makes them possible, obtainable and lasting.

Message for World Youth Day, 1992

ॐ

JUSTICE
AND EQUALITY

Freedom in justice will bring a new dawn of hope for the present generation as it has done before: for the homeless, for the unemployed, for the aging, for the sick and the handicapped, for the migrants and the undocumented workers, for all who hunger for human dignity in this land and in the world.

Address, New York, 1979

The question of *human dignity is particularly linked with efforts on behalf of justice.* Any violation of justice anywhere is an affront to human dignity, and all effective contributions to justice are truly worthy of the greatest praise. The purification of structures in the political, social, and economic fields cannot help but yield salutary results.

Address, Rome, 1980

In the face of serious forms of social and economic injustice and political corruption affecting entire peoples and nations, there is a growing reaction of indignation on the part of very many people whose fundamental human rights have been trampled upon and held in contempt, as well as an ever more widespread and acute sense of *the need for a radical* personal and social *renewal* capable of ensuring justice, solidarity, honesty, and openness.

Splendor Veritatis, 98

༄

This is the freedom that America is called to live and guard and to transmit. She is called to exercise it in such a way that it will also benefit the cause of freedom in other nations and among other peoples. The only true freedom, the only freedom that can truly satisfy is the freedom to do what we ought as human beings created by God according to his plan. It is *the freedom to live the truth of what we are and who we are* before God, the truth of our identity as children of God, as brothers and sisters in a common humanity. That is why Jesus Christ linked truth and freedom together, stating solemnly: "You will know the truth and the truth will set you free" (Jn. 8:32). All people are called to recognize the liberating truth of the sovereignty of God over them both as individuals and as nations.

Address, Miami, 1987

༄

. . . The effective and guaranteed observance of respect for human dignity and human rights will be impossible if individuals and communities do not overcome self-interest, fear, greed, and the thirst for power.

Address, Manila, 1995

ॐ

Man *affirms himself most completely by giving of himself.* This is the fulfillment of the commandment of love. This is also the full truth about man, a truth that Christ taught us by His life, and that the tradition of Christian morality, no less than the tradition of saints and of the many heroes of love of neighbor, took up and lived out in the course of history.

If we deprive *human freedom* of this possibility, if man does not commit himself to becoming a gift for others, then his freedom can become dangerous. It will become freedom to do what I myself consider as good, what brings me a profit or pleasure, even a sublimated pleasure. *If we cannot accept the prospect of giving ourselves as a gift, then the danger of a selfish freedom will always be present.*

Crossing the Threshold of Hope

ॐ

We can and must immediately reach out and display to the world our unity in proclaiming the mystery of Christ, in revealing the divine dimension as well as the human dimension, of the Redemption; and in struggling with unwearying perseverance for the dignity that each human being has reached and can continually reach in Christ.

Redemptor Hominis, 11

꒳

Immense distress moves us to launch a cry of alarm. Where is love for those who have been refused the right to live? For those who have been killed, mutilated, or imprisoned because they roam the streets? For those who have been exploited at an early age in forced labor or the commerce of perversion? For those whom famine has thrown on the roads of exile? For those who have been made to carry arms? Where is love for those who have been left without school education and have been condemned to illiteracy? Where is love for those whose family has been destroyed or displaced?

Address, Rome, 1993

꒳

The dignity of the person constitutes *the foundation of the equality of all people among themselves.* As a result, all forms of discrimination are totally unacceptable, especially those forms which unfortunately continue to divide and degrade the human family: from those based on race or economics to those social and cultural, from political or geographic, etc. Each discrimination constitutes an absolutely intolerable injustice, not so much for the tensions and the conflicts that can be generated in the social sphere . . . as for the dishonor inflicted on the dignity of the individual who is the victim of the injustice, but still more to the one who commits the injustice.

Christifideles Laici, 37

༕

On the one hand, the various declarations of human rights and the many initiatives inspired by these declarations show that at the global level there is a growing moral sensitivity more alert to acknowledging the value and dignity of every individual as a human being, without any distinction of race, nationality, religion, political opinion, or social class. On the other hand, these noble proclamations are unfortunately contradicted by a tragic repudiation of them in practice. This denial is still more distressing, indeed more scandalous, precisely because it is occurring in a society which makes the affirmation and protection of human rights its primary objective and its boast. How can these repeated affirmations of principle be reconciled with the continual increase and widespread justification of attacks on human life? How can we reconcile these declarations with the refusal to accept those who are weak and needy, or elderly, or those who have just been conceived?

Evangelium Vitae, 18

༕

This is our commitment. We would risk causing the victims of the most atrocious deaths to die again if we do not have an ardent desire for justice, if we do not commit ourselves, each according to his own capacities, to ensure that evil does not prevail over good as it did for millions of the children of the Jewish nation.

We must therefore redouble our efforts to free man from the specter of racism, exclusion, alienation, slavery, and xenophobia; to uproot these evils which are creeping into society and undermining the foundations of peaceful human coexistence. Evil always appears in new forms; it has many facets and its flattery is multiple. It is our task to unmask its dangerous power and neutralize it with God's help.

Address, Rome, 1994

✧

Just as personal dignity is the foundation of equality of all people among themselves, so it is also *the foundation of participation and solidarity of all people among themselves:* dialogue and communion are rooted ultimately in what people "are," first and foremost, rather than on what people "have."

Christifideles Laici, 37

✧

Recognizing the importance of a free exchange of ideas and information, the Church supports freedom of speech and of the press. At the same time, she insists that "the rights of individuals, families and society itself to privacy, public decency and the protection of basic values" demand to be respected. Public authorities are invited to set and enforce reasonable ethical standards for programming which will foster the human and religious values on which family life is built, and will discourage whatever is harmful. They should also encourage dialogue between the television industry and the public, providing structures and forums to make this possible.

Address, Rome, 1994

ॐ

W hen the individual is not recognized and loved in the person's dignity as the living image of God . . . the human being is exposed to more humiliating and degrading forms of "manipulation," that most assuredly reduce the individual to a slavery to those who are stronger. "Those who are stronger" can take a variety of names: an ideology, economic power, political and inhumane systems, scientific technocracy, or the intrusiveness of the mass-media. Once again we find ourselves before many persons—our sisters and brothers—whose fundamental rights are being violated, owing to their exceedingly great capacity for endurance and to the clear injustice of certain civil laws; the right to a house and to work; the right to a family and responsible parenthood; the right to participation in public and political life; the right to free-dom of conscience and the practice of religion.

Christifideles Laici, 5

☙

The perception of human dignity is certainly a meet-ing point for Christian thought and the best instances of contemporary culture. This dignity is based on the interior dimension of the human being created "in the image of God" (Gen. 1:26). In fact, among all the beings of the visible world, man alone is not confined to existing, but also knows that he exists, with his intellect, by means of which he "shares in the light of the divine mind" (*Gaudium et Spes,* n. 15).

Address, Rome, 1993

☙

In the past, and even to this day, there have been so many programs promising "healing" for the world and proclaiming the arrival of "true" justice in men's dealings with one another. But none of these can be regarded as complete unless it is linked with the justi-fication before God—which is the main foundation of all justice. . . .

Sign of Contradiction, **10.1**

☙

Bear genuine hope to the poor, who, inspired by their supernatural faith, look to the Church as their sole defense. . . . Blaze trails of hope and authentic liberation . . . as you continue to toil, dear brothers, in the closest union, for the authentic liberation that comes to us from Jesus Christ, the Redeemer of Man, which must be defended from ideologies alien to it, ideologies that evacuate its evangelical content.

Address to the Colombian Bishops, 1987

જ્જ

The right to life does not depend on a particular religious conviction. It is a primary, natural, inalienable right that springs from the very dignity of every human being. The defense of life from the moment of conception until natural death is the defense of the human person in the dignity that is his or hers from the sole fact of existence, independently of whether that existence is planned or welcomed by the persons who give rise to it.

Address, Rome, 1992

જ્જ

The fundamental criterion for comparing social, economic, and political systems . . . must be the humanistic criterion, namely the measure in which each system is really capable of reducing, restraining, and eliminating as far as possible the various forms of exploitation of man and of ensuring for him, through work, not only the just distribution of the indispensable material goods, but also a participation in

keeping with his dignity, in the whole process of production.

Peace Through Justice, 16

ॐ

A freedom which claims to be absolute ends up
treating the human body as a raw datum, devoid of
any meaning and moral values until freedom has
shaped it in accordance with its design. Consequently, human nature and the body appear as *pre-
suppositions or preambles,* materially *necessary* for
freedom to makes its choice, yet extrinsic to the person, the subject, and the human act. Their functions
would not be able to constitute reference points for
moral decisions, because the finality of these inclinations would be merely *"physical"* goods, called by
some "pre-moral."

Splendor Veritatis, 48

ॐ

Among all other earthly beings, *only a man or a
woman is a "person," a conscious and free being* and,
precisely for this reason, the "center and summit" of
all that exists on the earth.

Christifideles Laici, 37

ॐ

Although punishment in itself causes suffering, humiliation, deprivation of freedom—things which
grievously wound a man—it nevertheless serves a

good purpose (or at least it should) in that it restores justice and good order and helps to rehabilitate the offender, leads to his purification. We all know from present-day experience how the whole system of crime and punishment can lead to abuses, how "the good of society" is made the excuse for judging and condemning men not for any wrongdoing but for their disagreement with the tenets of the system, or often simply because they are misfits. We have all heard about terrible indictments—sometimes followed later by rehabilitation—and sentences inflicted on people disgracefully liquidated in the name, so it is said, of law and order. Nonetheless, these abuses cannot change the basic truth about punishment. Unjust application of judicial systems on the part of men only underlines the need for ultimate justice, the justice of God himself.

Sign of Contradiction, **19.2**

༨

Do not let this hour pass without renewing your commitment to action for social justice and peace. Turn to the Gospel of Jesus Christ to strengthen your resolve to become instruments for the common good! Learn from the Gospel that you have been entrusted with the justice and peace of God! We are not merely the builders of justice according to the standards of this world, but we are the bearers of the life of God, who is himself justice and peace! Let your endeavors to achieve justice and peace in all the spheres of your lives be a manifestation of God's love!

Address, Detroit, 1987

⁓

But the options and the illumination Christians need in the area of human promotion and liberation, especially that of the very neediest, can only be made according to the example of Jesus and obtained in the light of the Gospel, which forbids recourse to methods of hatred and violence. Love, and a preferential option for the poor, must not be exclusive or excluding. Love for the poor does not mean regarding the poor as a class, let alone as a class caught up in a struggle, or as a Church, separated from communion with and obedience to the shepherds appointed for them by Christ. Love, and the preferential option for the poor, must be implemented in the context of a conceptualization of the human being in his earthly and eternal calling.

Address, Medellín, Colombia, 1980

⁓

Besides wages, various social benefits intended to ensure the life and health of workers and their families play a part here. The expenses involved in health care, especially in the case of accidents at work, demand that medical assistance should be cheap or even free of charge. Another sector regarding benefits is the sector associated with the right to rest. In the first place this involves a regular weekly rest comprising at least Sunday and also a longer period of rest, namely the holiday or vacation taken once a year or possibly in several shorter periods during the year. A third sector concerns the right to a pension and to insurance for old age and in case of accidents at work.

Laborem Exercens, 19

✧

Patterned on God's freedom, man's freedom is not negated by his obedience to the divine law; indeed, only through this obedience does it abide in the truth and conform to human dignity.

Splendor Veritatis, 42

✧

Besides the acceptance of legal formulas safeguarding the principle of freedom of the human spirit, such as freedom of thought and expression, religious freedom and freedom of conscience, structures of social life exist in which the practical exercise of these freedoms condemns man, in fact if not formally, to become a second class or third class citizen, to see compromised his chances of social advancement, his professional career or his access to certain posts of responsibility, and to lose even the possibility of educating his children freely. It is a question of the highest importance that in internal social life, as well as international life, *all human beings* in every nation and country *should be able to enjoy effectively their full rights under any political regime or system.*

Only the safeguarding of this real completeness of rights for every human being without discrimination can ensure peace at its very roots.

Address to the UN, 1979

༄

The dignity of the person is the indestructible property of *every human being.* The force of this affirmation is based on the *uniqueness and irrepeatability of every person.* From it flows that the individual can never be reduced by all that seeks to crush and to annihilate the person into the anonymity that comes from collectivity, institutions, structures, and systems. As an individual, a person is not a number or simply a link in a chain, nor even less, an impersonal element in some system.

Christifideles Laici, 37

༄

In the life of every nation, social progress and human development are ensured by the respect given to the rights of the human person. The human person's very existence in dignity and his or her rightful participation in the life of the community are safeguarded by the deep respect that every person entertains for the dignity and the rights of every fellow human being.

In the same way, respect for the rights of peoples and nations must safeguard the existence in liberty of every nation and thus make possible its rightful and effective participation in all aspects of international life. Without this, it would be impossible to speak about solidarity. In order to be capable of global solidarity, *nations must* first of all *respect the human rights of their citizens* and in turn be recognized by their people as the expression of their sovereignty; secondly, *nations must respect the full rights of their fellow nations* and know also that their rights as a nation will not be disavowed.

Address, Detroit, 1987

ॐ

The dignity of the person is manifested in all its radiance when the person's origin and destiny are considered: created by God in his image and likeness as well as redeemed by the most precious blood of Christ, the person is called to be a "child in the Son" and a living temple of the Spirit, destined for the eternal life of blessed communion with God. For this reason every violation of the personal dignity of the human being cries out in vengeance to God and is an offense against the Creator of the individual.

Christifideles Laici, 37

ॐ

The successor of Peter presents himself here also as a witness to the immensity of human suffering, a witness to the almost apocalyptic menaces looking over the nations and mankind as a whole. He is trying to embrace these sufferings with his own weak human heart.

Address, Fátima, 1982

ༀ

Do not forget the needs of your homelands. Heed the cry of the poor and the oppressed in the countries and continents from which you come. Be convinced that the Gospel is the only path of genuine liberation and salvation for the world's peoples: "Your salvation, O Lord, is for all the peoples" (Responsorial Psalm, Ps. 95).

Address, Denver, Colorado, 1993

ༀ

LOVE

Only a person can love and only a person can be loved.

Mulieris Dignitatem, **29**

⌘

Love is true when *it creates the good of persons and of communities;* it creates that good and *gives it* to others. Only the one who is able to be demanding with himself in the name of love can also demand love from others. Love is demanding. It makes demands in all human situations; it is even more demanding in the case of those who are open to the Gospel. Is this not what Christ proclaims in "his" commandment? Nowadays people need to rediscover this demanding love, for it is the truly firm foundation of the family, a foundation able to "endure all things."

Letter to Families, **14**

⌘

Love is not an adventure. It has a taste of the whole man. It has his weight. And the weight of his whole fate. It cannot be a single moment. Man's eternity passes through it. That is why it is to be found in the dimensions of God, because only He is eternity.

Man looking out into time. To forget, to forget. To be for a moment only, only now—and cut oneself off from eternity. To take in everything at one moment and lose everything immediately after. Ah, the curse of that next moment and all the moments that follow, moments through which you will look for the way back to the moment that has passed, to have it once more, and through it—everything.

The Jeweler's Shop, **Act II**

～

God loves you all, without distinction, without limit. He loves those of you who are elderly, who feel the burden of the years. He loves those of you who are sick, those of you who are suffering from AIDS and from AIDS-related complex. He loves the relatives and friends of the sick and those who care for them. He loves us all with an unconditional and everlasting love.

Address, San Francisco, 1987

～

Love is a force, the driving force in salvation. Man—even the man who is far distant from the Gospel—is capable of recognizing the close tie between love and salvation. The concentration camps will always remain in men's minds as real-life symbols of hell-upon-earth; they expressed to the highest degree the evil that man is capable of inflicting on his fellow men. In one such camp Fr. Maximilian Kolbe died in 1941. All the prisoners knew that he died of his own free choice, offering his own life in exchange for that of a fellow-prisoner. And with that particular revelation there passed through that hell-upon-earth a breath of fearless and indestructible goodness, a kind of intimation of salvation. One man died, but humanity was saved! So close is the tie between love and salvation.

Sign of Contradiction, **6.2**

જ

Lord, grant us patience, serenity and courage; grant us to live in joyful charity, for love of You, with those who are suffering more than ourselves and with those who, though not suffering, have not a clear view of the meaning of life.

Address, Leper Colony, Marituba, Brazil, 1980

જ

Love includes the human body, and the body is made a sharer in spiritual love. . . . Consequently, sexuality, by means of which man and woman give themselves to one another through the acts which are proper and exclusive to spouses, is by no means something purely biological, but concerns the innermost being of the human person, as such. It is realized in a truly human way only if it is an integral part of the love by which a man and a woman commit themselves totally to one another until death.

Familiaris Consortio, **11**

✧

Man cannot live without love. He remains a being that is incomprehensible for himself, his life is senseless, if love is not revealed to him, if he does not encounter love, if he does not experience it and make it his own, if he does not participate intimately in it.

Redemptor Hominis, **10**

✧

The vocation to love, understood as true openness to our fellow human beings and solidarity with them, is the most basic of all vocations. It is the origin of all vocations in life.

Address, Manila, 1995

✧

"To carry out the commandment of love means accomplishing all the duties of the Christian family: fidelity and conjugal virtue, responsible parenthood and eduction. The 'little Church'—the domestic Church—means the family living in the spirit of the commandment of love, its interior truth, its daily toil, its spiritual beauty and its power." But to live this poem of love and unity in this way, you absolutely need to pray. In this

sense prayer becomes really essential for love and unity: in fact, prayer strengthens, relieves, purifies, exalts, helps to find light and advice, deepens the respect that spouses in particular must mutually nourish for their hearts, their consciences, and their bodies, by means of which they are so close to each other.

Address, Rome, 1981

⤳

Brothers, I love you as you are and for what you are. I should like one day to commune with you in the same chalice of the blood of Jesus Christ, filled with the faith of the Spirit.

"Appeal for Christian Unity," 1981

⤳

. . . I am appealing to you, who are concerned for the good of your own people and of all humanity. It is very important not to weaken man, his sense of the sacredness of life, his capacity for love and self-sacrifice.

Letter to the Leaders of the World, 1994

⤳

Love, an uncreated gift, is part of the inner mystery of God and is the very nucleus of theology. In creation and in the covenant love is made manifest not only as motive but also as fact, as reality, a consequence of divine working. Precisely for this reason, the world that emerged from the hands of God the Creator is itself structured on a basis of love. To be something created is to be something "endowed," above all with existence and, together with existence, nature—which reflects different levels of being, differing degrees of perfection and good in the world, from inferior beings to more perfect ones, although St. Thomas [Aquinas] declares that every being is perfect according to its kind.

Sign of Contradiction, 7.1

༄

Love for truth must be expressed in love for justice and in the resulting commitment to establishing the truth in relation within human society; nor can subjects be lacking in love for the law and the judicial system, which represent the human attempt to provide concrete norms for resolving practical cases.

Address, Rome, 1994

༄

Although man instinctively loves life because it is a good, this love will find further inspiration and strength, and new breadth and depth, in the divine dimensions of this good. Similarly, the love which every human being has for life cannot be reduced simply to a desire to have sufficient space for self-expression and for entering into relationships with others; rather, it develops in a joyous awareness that life can become the "place" where God manifests himself, where we meet him and enter into communion with him. The life which Jesus gives in no way lessens the value of our existence in time; it takes it and directs it to its final destiny: "I am the resurrection and the life . . . Whoever lives and believes in me shall never die" (Jn. 11:25–26).

Evangelium Vitae, **38**

⚬

A Christian who has not learned to see and love Christ in his neighbor is not fully Christian. We are our brothers' keepers; we are bound to each other by the bond of love . . .

Insegnamenti **IV,** 1, 476–77

⚬

Love is the power that gives rise to dialogue, in which we listen to each other and learn from each other. Love gives rise, above all, to the dialogue of prayer in which we listen to God's word, which is alive in the Holy Bible and alive in the life of the Church. Let love then build the bridge across our differences and at times our contrasting positions. Let love for each other and love for truth be the answer to polarization, when factions are formed because of differing views in matters that relate to faith or to the priorities for action. No one in the ecclesial community should ever feel alienated or unloved, even when tensions arise in the course of the common efforts to bring the fruits of the Gospel to society around us. Our unity as Christians, as Catholics, must always be a unity of love in Jesus Christ our Lord.

Address, Chicago, 1979

༕

Love increases by means of the truth, and truth draws near to the person by the help of love.

Insegnamenti V, 2, 1942

༕

There is no true freedom where life is not welcomed and loved; and there is no fullness of life except in freedom. Both realities have something inherent and specific which links them, inextricably: the vocation to love. Love, as a sincere gift of self, is what gives the life and freedom of the person their truest meaning.

Evangelium Vitae, 96

༕

The "living flame of love," of which Saint John [of the Cross] speaks, is above all a purifying fire. The mystical nights described by this great Doctor of the Church on the basis of his own experience correspond, in a certain sense, to purgatory. God makes man pass through such an interior purgatory of his sensual and spiritual nature in order to bring him into union with Himself. Here we do not find ourselves before a mere tribunal. We present ourselves before the power of Love itself.

Crossing the Threshold of Hope

෨

Christian truth cannot be assimilated without charity. Only if we reestablish among ourselves and constantly enrich a real climate of fraternal charity, can we make progress in the truth. Indeed, in so far as we are guided by the Spirit of truth, who is the fount of all fraternal charity and who manifests himself in this fraternal charity, can we understand the truth revealed to us; only his light can guide us to the whole truth.

Insegnamenti **VIII, 1, 1994**

෨

We have to accept the fact that love weaves itself into our fate.
If fate does not split the love, people win their victory,
But nothing else besides—and nothing above, either.
These are the limits of man.

The Jeweler's Shop, **Act III**

෨

Jesus left us love as his commandment. Love was to be the main prop and stay of the spiritual identity of his followers as they faced the hatred which at various times and in various forms was to be hurled at them by the world. "If the world hates you, know that before hating you it hated me" (Jn. 15:18).

Charity. Love. The fount and fullness of God's glory in man and man's glory in God.

Sign of Contradiction, **20.4**

☞

When life is challenged by conditions of hardship, maladjustment, sickness, or rejection, other programs—such as communities for treating drug addiction, residential communities for minors or the mentally ill, care and relief centers for AIDS patients, associations for solidarity especially toward the disabled—are eloquent expressions of what charity is able to devise in order to give everyone new reasons for hope and practical possibilities for life.

Evangelium Vitae, **88**

☞

In our age we are witnesses of a terrible exploitation of these words: love and freedom. The real meaning of these words—love and freedom—must be found again. I tell you: you must return to the Gospel. You must return to the school of Christ. Then you will transmit these spiritual goods: the sense of justice in all human relationships, the promotion and safeguarding of peace. And I tell you again, they are words that have been exploited, exploited many, many times. It is always necessary to return to the school of Christ, to find again the true, full and deep meaning of these words.

Address, Turin, 1980

❧

Love is formed in the human person, embraces body and soul, matures in the heart and in the will; to be "human," love must comprise the person in his physical, psychical, and spiritual totality.

Address, Rome, 1981

❧

God's salvation is the work of a love greater than man's sin. Love alone can wipe out sin and liberate from sin. Love alone can consolidate man in the good: in the unalterable and eternal good.

Insegnamenti V, 3, 1623

❧

Love of neighbor would mean above all and even exclusively respect for his freedom to make his own decisions.

Splendor Veritatis, 47

❧

MODERN WORLD

Man has need to develop his spirit and his conscience. This is often lacking to the man of today. . . . Man is a spiritual being. We, believers, know that we do not live in a closed world. We believe in God. We are worshipers of God. We are seekers of God.

Address, Morocco, 1985

༺

The enormous development of *biological and medical science,* united to an amazing *power in technology,* today provides possibilities on the very frontier of human life which imply new responsibilities. In fact, today humanity is in the position not only of "observing" but even "exercising a control over" human life at its very beginning and in its first stages of development.

Christifideles Laici, 38

༺

. . . While the climate of widespread moral uncertainty can in some way be explained by the multiplicity and gravity of today's social problems, and these can sometimes mitigate the subjective responsibility of individuals, it is no less true that we are confronted by an ever larger reality, which can be described as a veritable structure of sin. This reality is characterized by the emergence of a culture which denies solidarity and in many cases takes the form of a veritable "culture of death." This culture is actively fostered by powerful cultural, economic, and political currents which encourage an idea of society excessively concerned with efficiency.

Evangelium Vitae, 12

ﾋﾞ

The course of history—in our own day especially, perhaps—shows an ever-greater contrast between man's enormous material gains and his moral shortcomings, his falling-short in the sphere of what he is. One can quite safely say that in the sphere of what he is man fails to match what he possesses.

Sign of Contradiction, 18.2

ﾋﾞ

The man of today seems ever to be under threat from what he produces, that is to say from the result of the work of his hands and, even more so, of the work of his intellect and the tendencies of his will. All too soon, and often in an unforeseeable way, what this manifold activity of man yields is not only subjected to "alienation," in the sense that it is simply taken away from the person who produces it, but rather it turns against man himself, at least in part, through the indirect consequences of its effects returning on himself. It is or can be directed against him. This seems to make up the main chapter of the drama of present-day human existence in its broadest and universal dimension.

Redemptor Hominis, 15

৵

Suffering is a reality that is terribly real and sometimes even atrocious and heartrending. Physical, moral, and spiritual pain torments poor mankind at all times. We must be grateful to science, technology, medicine, and social and civil organizations which try in all ways to eliminate or at least assuage suffering: but it always remains victorious and the defeat weighs on afflicted and helpless man. It almost seems, in fact, that to greater social progress there corresponds a moral decline, with the consequence of other sufferings, fears, and concerns.

Address, Rome, 1979

৵

A critical analysis of our modern civilization shows that in the last hundred years it has contributed as never before to the development of material goods, but that it has also given rise, both in theory and still more in practice, to a series of attitudes in which *sensitivity to the spiritual dimension of human existence is diminished* to a greater or lesser extent, as a result of certain premises which reduce the meaning of human life chiefly to the many different material and economic factors—I mean to the demands of production, the market, consumption, the accumulation of riches or the growing bureaucracy with which an attempt is made to regulate these very processes. Is this not the result of having subordinated man to one single conception and sphere of values?

Address to the UN, 1979

❧

I know you are aware that, however much the joint responsibility of all in society is maintained and grows constantly, still, the initiation and control by human reason of the vital processes depends to a great extent upon those who have been chosen to govern; aware that disinterest and discernment must go side by side in order to remove from the exercise of your mission any pernicious confusions; above all, concerning the truth about man, with partial, destructive, and misguided views of his total reality; and also concerning authentic human solidarity, and any manipulations of the same in the interests of hidden individuals and against those of man.

Address, Lisbon, Portugal, 1982

❧

Indeed there is already a real perceptible anger that, while man's dominion over the world of things is making enormous advances, he should lose the essential threads of his dominion and in various ways let his humanity be subjected to the world and become himself something subject to manipulation in many ways—even if the manipulation is often not perceptible directly—through the whole of the organization of community life, through the production system, and through pressure from the means of social communication. Man cannot relinquish himself or the place in the visible world that belongs to him; he cannot become the slave of things, the slave of economic systems, the slave of production, the slave of his own products. A civilization purely materialistic in outline condemns man to such slavery, even if at times, no doubt, this occurs contrary to the intentions and the very premises of its pioneers. The present solicitude for man certainly has at its roots this problem. It is not a matter here merely of giving an abstract answer to the question: Who is man? It is a matter of the whole of the dynamism of life and civilization. It is a matter of the meaningfulness of the various initiatives of everyday life and also of the premises for many civilization programs, political programs, economic ones, social ones, state ones, and many others.

Redemptor Hominis, 16

The recent stage of human history, especially that of certain societies, brings a correct affirmation of technology as a basic coefficient of economic progress; but, at the same time, this affirmation has been accompanied by and continues to be accompanied by the raising of essential questions concerning human work in relationship to its subject, which is man. These questions are particularly charged with *content and tension of an ethical and social character.* They therefore constitute a continual challenge for institutions of many kinds, for states and governments, for systems and international organizations; they also constitute a challenge for the Church.

Laborem Exercens, 5

ॐ

. . . In the face of the modern world's development, *there is an ever-increasing number of people who ask themselves or who feel more keenly the most essential questions: What is man?* What is the meaning of suffering, of evil, of death, which persist despite all progress? What are these victories, purchased at so high a cost, really worth? What can man offer to society and what can he expect from it? What will there be after this life? The Church believes that Christ, who died and was resurrected for the sake of all, continuously gives to man through His Spirit the light and the strength to respond to his higher destiny. Nor is there any other name under heaven given to the human race by which we are to be saved.

Crossing the Threshold of Hope

ॐ

The contemporary world, in spite of enormous scientific and technical progress, lives in terror of a great catastrophe which could overturn its grand successes if war should prevail over peace. For this reason, expenditures for armaments should be reduced, to guarantee all countries a minimum of conditions necessary to worldwide development, especially with regard to the agricultural and food sector. The state of absolute poverty of certain groups of human beings in many countries with less developed economies offends the dignity of millions of persons forced to live in conditions of degrading misery. It is therefore urgent to give to workers in the fields the opportunity to realize concretely their basic human rights.

Address, Vila Vicosa, 1982

ॐ

Perhaps one of the most glaring weaknesses of present day civilization lies in an adequate view of the human being. Undoubtedly our age is the age . . . when human values have been trodden underfoot as never before.

Address at the Puebla Conference, 1979

ॐ

Whole countries and nations where religion and the Christian life were formerly flourishing and capable of fostering a viable and working community of faith are now put to a hard test, and in some cases are even undergoing a radical transformation as a result of a constant spreading of an indifference to religion, of secularism and atheism. This particularly concerns countries and nations of the so-called First World in which economic well-being and consumerism, even if coexistent with a tragic situation of poverty and misery, inspires and sustains a life lived "as if God did not exist." This indifference to religion and the practice of religion devoid of true meaning in the face of life's very serious problems are not less worrying and upsetting when compared with declared atheism.

Christifideles Laici, 34

ॐ

By the year 2000 we need to be more united, more willing to advance along the path toward the unity for which Christ prayed on the eve of His Passion. This unity is enormously precious. In a certain sense, the future of the world is at stake. The future of the Kingdom of God in the world is at stake. Human weaknesses and prejudices cannot destroy God's plan for the world and for humanity. If we appreciate this, we can look to the future with a certain *optimism*. We can trust that "the one who began this good work in us will bring it to completion" (cf. Phil. 1:6).

Crossing the Threshold of Hope

ॐ

We are living in an age in which the whole world proclaims freedom of conscience and religious freedom, and also in an age in which the battle against religion—defined as "the opium of the people"—is being fought in such a way as to avoid, as far as possible, making any new martyrs. And so the program for today is one of face-saving persecutions: persecution is declared nonexistent and full religious freedom is declared assured. What is more, this program has succeeded in giving many people the impression that it is on the side of Lazarus against the rich man, that it is therefore on the same side as Christ, whereas in fact it is above all against Christ. Can we really say: "above all"? We would so much like to be able to affirm the opposite. But unfortunately the facts demonstrate clearly that the battle against religion *is* being fought, and that this battle still constitutes an untouchable point of dogma in the program.

Sign of Contradiction, 22.1

ॐ

Man . . . lives increasingly in fear. He is afraid that what he produces—not all of it, of course, or even most of it, but part of it and precisely that part that contains a special share of his genius and initiative— can radically turn against himself; he is afraid that it can become the means and instrument for an unimaginable self-destruction, compared with which all the cataclysms and catastrophes of history known to us seem to fade away. This gives rise to a question: Why is it that the power given to man from the beginning by which he was to subdue the earth turns against himself, producing an understandable state of disquiet, of conscious or unconscious fear and menace, which in various ways is being communicated to the whole of the present-day human family and is manifesting itself under various aspects?

Redemptor Hominis, 15

ॐ

While secularism attributes to earthly things their due and rightful autonomy, secularism insists that the world must be taken away from God! And then? Then everything must be given to man! But can the world really be given to man more fully than it was given to him at the start of creation? Can it be given to him in a different way? Can it be given independently of the objective order of being? of good? of evil? And supposing it were given in a different way, independently, that is, of the objective order, might it not rebound on man, reducing him to slavery? Might it not turn him into a mere tool?

Sign of Contradiction, 4.3

ॐ

MORALITY

Human acts are moral acts because they express and determine the goodness or evil of the individual who performs them. They do not produce a change merely in the state of affairs outside of man but, to the extent that they are deliberate choices, they give moral definition to the very person who performs them, determining his *profound spiritual traits*. This was perceptively noted by Saint Gregory of Nyssa: "All things subject to change and to becoming never remain constant, but continually pass from one state to another, for better or worse . . ."

Splendor Veritatis, 71

This century has so far been a century of great calamities for man, of great devastations, not only material ones but also moral ones, indeed, perhaps above all, moral ones.

Redemptor Hominis, 17

There is an even more profound aspect which needs to be emphasized: Freedom negates and destroys itself and becomes a factor leading to the destruction of others when it no longer recognizes and respects its essential link with the truth. When freedom, out of a desire to emancipate itself from all forms of tradition and authority, shuts out even the most obvious evidence of an objective and universal truth, which is the foundation of personal and social life, then the person ends up by no longer taking as the sole and indisputable point of reference for his own choices the truth about good and evil, but only his subjective and changeable opinion or, indeed, his selfish interest and whim.

Evangelium Vitae, 19

༠༠

According to St. Paul, conscience in a certain sense confronts man with the law and thus becomes a "witness" for man: a witness of his own faithfulness or unfaithfulness with regard to the law, of his essential moral rectitude or iniquity. Conscience is the only witness, since what takes place in the heart of the person is hidden from the eyes of everyone outside. Conscience makes its witness known only to the person himself. And, in turn, only the person himself knows what his own response is to the voice of conscience.

Veritatis Splendor, 57

༠༠

When . . . the Gospel and its message of salvation are rejected, a process of the erosion of moral values is begun, which easily has negative repercussions on the life of society itself. Is it perhaps not possible to see in this the ultimate reason for the failure of a culture based on personal gain, which does not take into consideration the real needs of the individual, especially those of the poor, condemned to remain the victims of the injustices of a society that is increasingly competitive and ever more lacking in solidarity?

Homily Against the Mafia, 1993

چ

All fields of human endeavor are enriched by true ethical values. During my pastoral journey I had occasion to speak of these values and to profess my own profound esteem for all who embrace them in national life. There is no sphere of activity that does not benefit when religious values are actively pursued. *The political, social, and economic domains are authenticated and reinforced by the application of those moral standards* that must be irrevocably incorporated into the tradition of every state.

Address, Rome, 1981

چ

Christian wisdom, which the Church teaches by divine authority, continuously inspires the faithful of Christ zealously to endeavor to relate human affairs and activities with religious values in a single living synthesis. Under the direction of these values all things are mutually connected for the glory of God and the integral development of the human person, a development that includes both corporeal and spiritual well-being.

. . . The cultural atmosphere in which a human being lives has a great influence upon his or her way of thinking and, thus, of acting. Therefore, a division between faith and culture is more than a small impediment to evangelization, while a culture penetrated with the Christian spirit is an instrument that favors the spreading of the Good News.

Sapientia Christiana, **Foreword**

༈

The moral goodness of all progress is measured by its genuine benefit to man, considered in relation to his twofold corporeal and spiritual dimension; as a result, justice is done to what man is; if the good were not linked to man, who must be its beneficiary, it might be feared that humanity were heading for its own destruction. The scientific community is ceaselessly called to keep the factors in order, situating scientific aspects within the framework of an integral humanism; in this way it will take into account the metaphysical, ethical, social, and juridical questions that conscience faces and which the principles of reason can clarify.

Address to Pontifical Academy of Sciences, Rome, 1994

ॐ

The *moral conscience* of humanity is not able to turn aside or remain indifferent in the face of these gigantic strides accomplished by a technology that is acquiring a continually more extensive and profound dominion over the working processes that govern procreation and the first phases of human life. Today as perhaps never before in history or in this field, *wisdom shows itself to be the only firm basis to salvation,* in that persons engaged in scientific research and its application are always to act with intelligence and love, that is, respecting, even remaining in veneration of the inviolable dignity of the personhood of every human being from the first moment of life's existence. This occurs when science and technology are committed with licit means to the defense of life and the cure of disease in its beginnings, refusing on the contrary—even for the dignity of research itself—to perform operations that result in falsifying the genetic patrimony of the individual and of human generative power.

Christifideles Laici, 38

ॐ

The essential sense of the state, as a political community, consists in that the society and people composing it are master and sovereign of their own destiny. This sense remains unrealized if, instead of the exercise of power with the moral participation of the society or people, what we see is the imposition of power by a certain group upon all the other members of society. This is essential in the present age, with its enormous increase in people's social awareness and the accompanying need for the citizens to have a right share in the political life of the community. . . .

Redemptor Hominis, 17

Scientific knowledge does not have its proper end in itself. It is at the service of man: of man-as-person, as well as of humanity as a whole, of man understood as humankind in its specific difference, characterized by the presence of spirit—knowledge, conscience, will—and by conscious and free activity. In regard to man, science can neither claim to be neutral nor act so. It is at once a gift that comes from on high, and an unceasing conquest of the spirit that seeks and finds, interprets and organizes. It has a liberating and elevating function, whenever it is not exercised—as is the case in the invention and use of lethal weapons—in the service of death rather than of life, for the benefit of the power of a few rather than in the service of the rights of all.

Address, University of Trieste, 1992

჻

The Mystery of Life, and of human life in particular, is attracting the increased attention of experts who are drawn by the extraordinary opportunities for investigation that scientific and technological advances offer their research today. While this new situation opens up fascinating horizons for intervention at the sources of life itself, it also gives rise to a variety of new moral questions that man cannot ignore without the risk of taking steps that could prove irreversible.

Apostolic Letter, 1994

჻

In our own day are we not perhaps witnesses of the fact that often in rich societies, where there is an abundance of material well-being, permissiveness and moral relativism find easy acceptance? And where the moral order is undermined, God is forgotten and questions of ultimate responsibility are set aside. *In such situations a practical atheism pervades private and public living.*

Address, Laguna Seca, California, 1987

჻

The moral life presents itself as the response due to the many gratuitous initiatives taken by God out of love for man. It is a response of love, according to the statement made in Deuteronomy about the fundamental commandment: "Hear O Israel: The Lord our God is one Lord; and you shall love the Lord your God with all your heart, and with all your soul, and with all your might. And these words which I command you this day shall be upon your heart; and you shall teach them diligently to your children" (Dt. 6:4–7). Thus the moral life, caught up in the gratuitousness of God's love, is called to reflect his glory.

Splendor Veritatis, 10

In modern society, ensuring a value-oriented education is without doubt the greatest challenge for the whole educational community. . . . A culture cannot be passed on without at the same time passing on its essential basis and its inmost soul, the truth and dignity of life and of the human person, who finds in God his origin and his end, revealed by Christ. Thus young people will discover the deep meaning of their lives, which will nourish their hope.

Address to Teachers, Rome, 1994

The de-Christianizing of society involves not only an increasing indifference to religion, a loss of faith, but also an obscuring of the moral sense.

Ad Limina **Address, 1993**

It would be an alarming symptom if a society should lose its sensitivity in such a way that an appeal to conscience becomes a license to kill another person, whether the child growing in its mother's womb or the elderly and terminally ill person whose life restricts that of another whose life is oriented to personal interests. Only a nation of egoists could dismiss the fact that a conscience worthy of its name always demands the prevention of death.

Ad Limina **Address, 1992**

PEACE AND WAR

In our modern world to refuse peace means not only to provoke the sufferings and the loss that—today more than ever—war, even a limited one, implies: it could also involve the total destruction of entire regions, not to mention the threat of possible or probable catastrophes in ever vaster and possibly even universal proportions.

**"Negotiation, The Only Realistic Solution
to the Continuing Threat of War," 2**

⟶⟵

If it is to be true and lasting, peace must be truly *human*. The desire for peace is universal. It is embedded in the hearts of all human beings, and it cannot be achieved unless the human person is placed at the center of every effort to bring about unity and brotherhood among nations.

Address, Washington, DC, 1979

⟶⟵

The Church is aware of the extreme seriousness of the situation created by the forces of division and war, which today constitute a grave threat not only to the balance and harmony of nations but to the very survival of humanity, and she feels it her duty to offer and suggest her own unique collaboration for the overcoming of conflicts and the restoration of concord.

Reconciliatio et Paenitentia, 25

જી

Those who are responsible for the life of peoples seem above all to be engaged in a frantic search for political means and technical solutions which would allow the results of eventual conflicts "to be contained." While having to recognize the limits of their efforts in this direction, they persist in believing that in the long run war is inevitable. Above all this is found in the specter of a possible military confrontation between the two major camps which divide the world today and continues to haunt the future of humanity.

Certainly no power, and no statesman, would be of a mind to admit to planning war or to wanting to take such an initiative. Mutual distrust, however, makes us believe or fear that because others might nourish designs or desires of this type, each, especially among the great powers, seems to envisage no other possible

solution than through necessity to prepare suffi-
ciently strong defense to be able to respond to an
eventual attack.

"Negotiation," 2

᪐

Authentic peace is only possible if the dignity of the
human person is promoted at every level of society,
and every individual is given the chance to live in
accordance with dignity.

Address, Rome, 1995

᪐

Alas, there are still rising today from this world too
many cries of despair and pain, the cries of our brothers and sisters in humanity, crushed by war, injustice,
unemployment, poverty, and loneliness.

Address, Rome, 1995

᪐

We are oppressed . . . by the sad picture of so many
brothers and sisters on earth who are dying of hunger, sickness, and drugs; we are grieved to notice the
dark fascination that various forms of violence still
exercise on the human heart; we are disturbed in particular when we notice the ease with which, even
today, people give in to the illusion that a just and
lasting peace can be born of war. When will men suc-

ceed in understanding that their dignity is degraded every time they do not do everything possible for peace to triumph and reign among peoples and nations?

Address, Rome, 1982

࿓

Perhaps no other question of our day touches so many aspects of the human condition as that of armaments and disarmament. There are questions on the scientific and technical level; there are social and economic questions. There are deep problems of a political nature that touch the relations between states and among peoples.

"Negotiation," 4

࿓

Courageous men and women, ready to look at one another and listen, will never be lacking. They will be capable of finding fitting tools for building societies where each person is absolutely necessary to the other, and where diversity is recognized above all source of enrichment. One does not write peace with letters of blood, but with the mind and the heart!

Address, Rome, 1995

࿓

As in the days of swords and spears, so too today in the era of missiles, more than arms, it is the human heart which kills.

Address, Erice, Italy, 1993

✧

Speaking of human suffering, my thought goes to all the painful events which depend on the bad will of unscrupulous men, who for ideological reasons or for the sake of profit give themselves up to forms of violence, which do not stop even in the face of those human situations which have been regarded as worthy of particular respect by every people and in all times.

General Audience, Rome, 1978

✧

At this time when in so many places the mounting, inhuman din of war is heard once again, our world needs believers who raise their voices forcefully to intercede for peace. The prayers offered during these days is joined to the cry of the oppressed and the desire of millions of men and women who want to live in peace and security.

Papal Letter to "Prayer Meeting for Peace," 1992

✧

. . . Today more than ever before mankind needs Christ, the Prince of Peace: the hearts of men are thirsting for His peace. The approach of the third Millennium offers all believers a further reason for apostolic endeavor.

Address, Rome, 1994

꒜

And how can we fail to consider the violence against life done to millions of human beings, especially children, who are forced into poverty, malnutrition, and hunger because of an unjust distribution of resources between peoples and between social classes? And what of the violence inherent not only in wars as such, but in the scandalous arms trade, which spawns the many armed conflicts which stain our world with blood? What of the spreading of death caused by reckless tampering of the world's ecological balance, by the criminal spread of drugs or by the promotion of certain kinds of sexual activity which, besides being morally unacceptable, also involve grave risks to life? It is impossible to catalogue completely the vast array of threats to human life, so many are the forms, whether explicit or hidden, in which they appear today!

Evangelium Vitae, 10

꒜

War is not inevitable; peace is possible! It is possible because man has a conscience and a heart. It is possible because God loves each one of us, just as each one is, so as to transform and make him or her grow.

Address, Rome, 1994

❦

. . . Divisions are seen in the relationships between individuals and groups, and also at the level of larger groups: nations against nations, and blocs of opposing countries, in a headlong quest for domination. At the root of this alienation it is not hard to discern conflicts which, instead of being resolved through dialogue, grow more acute in confrontation and opposition. Careful observers, studying the elements that cause division, discover reasons of the most widely differing kinds: from the growing disproportion between groups, social classes, and countries to ideological rivalries that are far from dead; from the opposition between economic interests to political polarization; from tribal differences to discrimination for social and religious reasons.

Reconciliatio et Paenitentia, 2

❦

Nothing is resolved by war. On the contrary, everything is placed in jeopardy by war.

Address, Rome, 1992

❦

. . . It is only when hatred and injustice are sanctioned and organized by the ideologies based on them, rather than on the truth about the human person, that they take possession of entire nations and drive them to act. . . . May the memory of those terrible events guide the actions of everyone, particularly the leaders of nations in our own time, when other forms of injustice are fueling new hatreds and when new ideologies which exalt violence are appearing on the horizon.

Centessimus Annus, 17

ও

Our worldwide arms systems impinge in great measure on cultural developments. But at the heart of them all there are present spiritual questions which concern the very identity of man, and his choices for the future and for generations yet to come. Sharing my thoughts with you, I am conscious of all the technical, scientific, social, economic, and political aspects, but especially of the ethical, cultural, and spiritual ones.

"Negotiation," 4

ও

In the face of the instruments of destruction and death, in the face of violence and cruelty, we have no other recourse but to God, with our words and with our hearts. We are neither strong nor powerful, but we know that God does not leave unanswered the entreaty of those who turn to Him with sincere faith, especially when the present and future destiny of millions of people is at stake.

Address, Rome, 1993

❧

. . . We are unable to overlook another phenomenon that is quite evident in present-day humanity: Perhaps as never before in history, humanity is daily buffeted by *conflict*. This is a phenomenon which has many forms, displayed in a legitimate plurality of mentalities and initiatives, but manifested in the fatal opposition of persons, groups, categories, nations, and blocks of nations. This opposition takes the form of violence, of terrorism, and of war. Once again, but with proportions enormously widespread, diverse sectors of humanity today, wishing to show their "omnipotence," renew the futile experience of constructing the "Tower of Babel" . . . which spreads confusion, struggle, disintegration, and oppression. The human family is thus in itself dramatically convulsed and wounded.

Christifideles Laici, 6

❧

An insane arms race swallowed up the resources needed for the development of national economies and for assistance to the less developed nations. Scientific and technological progress, which should have contributed to man's well-being, was transformed into an instrument of war: science and technology were directed to the production of ever more efficient and destructive weapons. Meanwhile, an ideology, a perversion of authentic philosophy, was called upon to provide doctrinal justification for the new war. And this war was not simply expected and prepared for, but was actually fought with enormous bloodshed in various parts of the world. The logic of power blocs or empires . . . led to a situation in which controversies and disagreements among Third World countries were systematically aggravated and exploited in order to create difficulties for the adversary.

Centessimus Annus, **17**

جب

What person of goodwill does not long for peace? Today, peace is universally recognized as one of the highest values to be sought and defended. And yet, as the specter of a deadly war between opposing ideological blocs fades away, grave local conflicts continue to engulf various parts of the world.

Address, Rome, 1992

جب

Ladies and gentlemen, the world will not be able to continue for long along this way. A conviction, which is at the same time a moral imperative, forces upon anyone who has become aware of the situation at stake, and who is also inspired by the elementary sense of responsibilities that are incumbent on every-one: consciences must be mobilized! The efforts of human consciences must be increased in proportion to the tension between good and evil to which men at the end of the twentieth century are subjected. We must convince ourselves of the priority of ethics over technology, of the primacy of the person over things, of the superiority of spirit over matter. . . . The cause of man will be served if science forms an alliance with conscience.

Address, Rome, 1980

༄

It is a complex and delicate dialogue of reconciliation in which the Church is engaged, especially through the work of the *Holy See* and its different *organisms*. The Holy See already endeavors to intervene with the leaders of nations and the heads of the various international bodies, or seeks to associate itself with them, conduct a dialogue with them and encourage them to dialogue with one another, for the sake of reconciliation in the midst of the many conflicts. It does this not for ulterior motives or hidden interests—since it has none—but "out of a humanitarian concern," placing its institutional structure and moral authority, which are altogether unique, at the service of concord and peace. It does this in the conviction that as "in war two parties rise against one another" so "in the question of peace there are also necessarily two parties which must know how to commit themselves," and in this "one finds the true meaning of a dialogue for peace."

Reconciliatio et Paenitentia, 25

ॐ

Among the signs of hope we should also count the spread at many levels of public opinion of a new sensitivity ever more opposed to war as an instrument for the resolution of conflicts between peoples and increasingly oriented to finding effective but "nonviolent" means to counter the armed aggressor.

Evangelium Vitae, 27

ॐ

In an area already tense and fraught with unavoidable dangers, there is no place for exaggerated speech or threatening stances. Indulgence in rhetoric, in inflamed and impassioned vocabulary, in veiled threat and scare tactics can only exacerbate a problem that needs sober and diligent examination. On the other hand, governments and their leaders cannot carry on the affairs of state independent of the wishes of their peoples. The history of civilization gives us stark examples of what happens when this is tried. Currently the fear and preoccupation of so many groups in various parts of the world reveal that people are more and more frightened about what would happen if irresponsible parties unleash some nuclear war.

"Negotiation," 7

↭

. . . Totally unsuppressible is that human longing experienced by individuals and whole peoples for the inestimable good of *peace* in justice. The Gospel Beatitude: "Blessed are the peacemakers" (Mt. 5:9) finds in the people of our time a new and significant resonance: entire populations today live, suffer, and labor to bring about peace and justice. The *participation* by so many persons and groups in the life of society is increasingly pursued today as the way to make a desired peace become a reality.

Christifideles Laici, 6

↭

PRAYER

Prayer is an act of hope. It is an expression of hope, the sign of hope for the world, for mankind. Prayer enables us, as the Apostle [St. Paul] says, to look towards the fulfillment of our hope, towards that reality to which the human heart aspires: "If we still hope for that which we do not see, patience assists us to wait for it" (Rom. 8:25).

Sign of Contradiction, 5.4

In prayer we express to God our feelings, our thoughts, our sentiments. We wish to love and to be loved, to be understood and to understand. Only God loves us perfectly, with an everlasting love. In prayer, we open our hearts and our minds to this God of love. And it is prayer that makes us one with the Lord. Through prayer we come to share more deeply in God's life and in his love.

Youth Rally, New Orleans, 1987

The family celebrates the Gospel of life through daily prayer, both individual prayer and family prayer. The family prays in order to glorify and give thanks to God for the gift of life, and implores his light and strength in order to face times of difficulty and suffering without losing hope. But the celebration which gives meaning to every other form of prayer and worship is found in the family's actual daily living together, if it is a life of love and self-giving.

Evangelium Vitae, 93

🙠

Prayer makes us aware that everything—even evil—finds its principal and definitive reference point in God.

Letter to U. S. Bishops, 1993

🙠

The transcendence of the human person manifests itself in the prayer of faith, but from time to time in profound silence too. This silence, which sometimes seems to separate man from God, is nonetheless a special manifestation of the vital bond linking God and the human spirit.

Sign of Contradiction, 2.4

🙠

Prayer increases the strength and spiritual unity of the family, helping the family to partake of God's own "strength." In the solemn nuptial blessing during the

Rite of Marriage, the celebrant calls upon the Lord in these words: "Pour out upon them [the newlyweds] the grace of the Holy Spirit so that by your love poured into their hearts they will remain faithful in the marriage covenant." This "visitation" of the Holy Spirit gives rise to the inner strength of families, as well as the power capable of uniting them in love and truth.

Letter to Families, 4

◛

In the silence of prayer, encounter with God is actuated.

Insegnamenti V, 3, 1138–40

◛

Prayer is always a wonderful reduction of eternity to the dimension in time, a reduction of the eternal wisdom to the dimension of human knowledge, feeling, and understanding, a reduction of the eternal Love to the dimension of the human heart, which at times is incapable of absorbing its riches and seems to break.

Sign of Contradiction, 17.3

◛

The Church prays for the suffering. Suffering, in fact, is always a great test not only of physical strength but also of spiritual strength. Saint Paul's truth about "completing the sufferings of Christ" (cf. Col. 1:24) is part of the Gospel. It contains the joy and the hope that are essential to the Gospel; but man will not cross the threshold of that truth without the help of the Holy Spirit. *Prayer for the suffering and with the suffering is therefore a special part of this great cry* that the Church and the Pope raise together with Christ. It is a cry for the victory of good even through evil, through suffering, through every wrong and human injustice.

Crossing the Threshold of Hope

ॐ

. . . The experience of prayer, as a basic act of the believer, is common to all religions, including those in which there is only a rather vague belief in a personal God or in which it is confused by false representations.

Address, Rome, 1992

ॐ

Prayer is indispensable for persevering in pursuit of the good, indispensable for overcoming the trials life brings to man owing to his weakness. Prayer is strength for the weak and weakness for the strong! Here is what the Apostle [St. Paul] has to say: "Thus the Spirit too comes to help us in our weakness, because we do not know how to ask for the right things; but the Spirit himself intercedes for us, with sighs that words cannot express" (Rom. 8:26). Prayer can be said to be a constitutive element of human existence in the world. Human existence is "being directed towards God." At the same time it is "being within the dimensions of God," a humble but courageous entering into the depths of God's thought, the depths of his mystery and his plans. It is a kind of drawing on the source of divine power: will and grace.

Sign of Contradiction, **15.4**

৵

Christian prayer, which we want to consider today, has its roots in the Old Testament. In fact, it is intimately connected with the religious experience of the people of Israel, for whom God chose to reserve the revelation of His mystery.

In contrast to the pagan peoples, the pious Israelite knew "the face" of God and could turn to Him in confidence in the name of the covenant made at the foot of Mount Sinai. In Israel Yahweh was prayed to as the creator of the universe, the master of human destiny, the one who performed the most extraordinary deeds. First and foremost, however, He was addressed as the God of the covenant.

Address, Rome, 1992

৵

In all human work prayer brings in a reference to God, Creator and Redeemer, and contributes at the same time to the total humanization of labor. Do not let yourselves be seduced by the temptation that man can truly find himself by turning his back on God, by canceling prayer from his life, and remaining nothing but a worker, deceiving himself that what he produces alone can fill the needs of the human heart.

Homily, Czestochowa, Poland, 1979

༃

Prayer particularly belongs to the Christian religion, in which it occupies a central position. Jesus urges us to "pray always without becoming weary" (Lk. 18:1). Christians know that for them prayer is as essential as breathing, and once they have tasted the sweetness of intimate conversation with God, they do not hesitate to immerse in it with trusting abandonment.

Address, Rome, 1992

༃

Prayer can truly change your life. For it turns your attention away from yourself and directs your mind and your heart toward the Lord. If we look only at ourselves, with our own limitations and sins, we quickly give way to sadness and discouragement. But if we keep *our eyes fixed on the Lord,* then our hearts are filled with hope, our minds are washed in the light of truth, and we come to know the fullness of the Gospel with all its promise and life.

Youth Rally, New Orleans, 1987

༃

Prayer is the place where, in a very simple way, the creative and fatherly remembrance of God is made manifest: not only man's remembrance of God, but also and especially God's remembrance of man.

Letter to Families, 10

༈

Man goes beyond himself by reaching out towards God, and thus progresses beyond the limits imposed on him by created things, by space and time, by his own contingency. The transcendence of the person is closely bound up with responsiveness to the one who himself is the touchstone for all our judgments concerning being, goodness, truth, and beauty. It is bound up with responsiveness to the one who is nevertheless totally Other, because he is infinite.

Sign of Contradiction, 2.4

༈

It is significant that precisely *in and through prayer, man comes to discover in a very simple and yet profound way his own unique subjectivity:* in prayer the human "I" more easily perceives the depth of what it means to be a person. *This is also true of the family,* which is not only the basic "cell" of society, but also possesses a particular subjectivity of its own. This subjectivity finds its first and fundamental confirmation, and is strengthened, precisely when the members of the family meet in the common invocation: "Our Father."

Letter to Families, 4

ॐ

The most powerful humanitarian intervention is always prayer. Prayer represents an enormous spiritual power, especially when accompanied by sacrifice and suffering. . . . Even if it is not apparent to a superficial glance and many people do not acknowledge it, prayer joined to sacrifice constitutes the most powerful force in human history.

Address, Rome, 1994

ॐ

We must have recourse to Him: You know that Christ is found in the personal dialogue of prayer and, especially, in the reality of the sacraments.

Audience, Rome, 1980

ॐ

There are several definitions of prayer. But it is most often called a talk, a conversation, a colloquy with God. Conversing with someone, not only do we speak, but we also listen. Prayer, therefore, is also listening. It consists of listening to hear the interior voice of grace. Listening to hear the call. And then as you ask me how the Pope prays, I answer you: Like every Christian, he speaks and he listens. Sometimes, he prays without words, and then he listens all the more. The most important thing is precisely what he "hears." And he also tries to unite prayer with his obligations, his activities, his work, and to unite his work with prayer. In this way, day after day, he tries to carry out his "service," his "ministry," which comes to him from the will of Christ and from the living tradition of the Church.

Address, Paris, 1980

જી

Everything human is profoundly affected by prayer. *Human work is revolutionized by prayer*, uplifted to its highest level. Prayer is the source of the full humanization of work. In prayer the value of work is understood, for we grasp the fact that we are truly collaborators of God in the transformation and elevation of the world. Prayer is the consecration of this collaboration. At the same time it is the means through which we face the problems of life and in which all pastoral endeavors are conceived and nurtured.

Ad Limina **Address, 1988**

જી

SIN AND
SALVATION

At the heart of every *situation of sin* are always to be found sinful people.

Reconciliatio et Paenitentia, 16

꙰

"Secularism" is by nature and definition a movement of ideas and behavior which advocates a humanism totally without God, completely centered upon the cult of action and production and caught up in the heady enthusiasm of consumerism and pleasure-seeking, unconcerned with the danger of "losing one's soul." This consumerism cannot but undermine the sense of sin. At the very most, sin will be reduced to what offends man. But it is precisely here that we are faced with the bitter experience . . . that man can build a world without God but this world will end by turning against him. In fact, God is the origin and the supreme end of man, and man carries in himself a divine seed.

Reconciliatio et Paenitentia, 18

～

The greater the penitent's moral misfortune, the greater should be the mercy shown.

Address, Rome, 1993

～

"*Ecce nova facio omnia*" [Behold I make all things new]. . . . This is the point in history when all men are so to speak "conceived" afresh and follow a new course within God's plan—the plan prepared by the Father in the truth of the Word and in the gift of Love. It is the point at which the history of mankind makes a fresh start, no longer dependent on human conditioning—if one may put it like that. This fresh starting-point belongs in the divine order of things, in the divine perspective on man and the world. The finite, human categories of time and space are almost completely secondary. All men, from the beginning of the world until its end, have been redeemed by Christ and his cross.

***Sign of Contradiction,* 10.2**

～

Jesus Christ is the eternal salvation which revealed itself in the fullness of time. He is the truth which sets free, the word which saves.

In order to communicate the Good News to all people, He founded His Church with the specific mission of evangelizing. After Pentecost, the Church enthusiastically obeyed her divine founder's command and began the mission of spreading the Good News of salvation.

Address, Rome, 1993

༯

Another reason for the disappearance of the sense of sin in contemporary society is to be found in the errors made in evaluating certain findings of the human sciences. Thus on the basis of certain affirmations of psychology, concern to avoid creating feelings of guilt or to place limits on freedom leads to a refusal ever to admit any shortcoming. Through an undue extrapolation of the criteria of the science of sociology, it finally happens—as I have already said—that all failings are blamed upon society, and the individual is declared innocent of them.

Reconciliatio et Paenitentia, 18

༯

Therefore, what is salvation? It is the victory of good over evil, achieved in man in all dimensions of his existence. The very overcoming of evil has already a salvific character. The definitive form of salvation for man will consist in being completely freed from evil and reaching the fullness of God. This fullness is called, and in fact is, eternal salvation. It is realized in the kingdom of God as an eschatological reality of eternal life.

Address, Lisbon, 1982

↜

The forgiveness of sins first experienced in baptism is a recurring need in the life of every Christian. Restoring a proper sense of sin is the first step to be taken in facing squarely the grave spiritual crisis looming over men and women today, a crisis which can well be described as "an eclipse of conscience." Without a healthy awareness of their own sinfulness, people will never experience the depth of God's redeeming love for them while they were still sinners (cf. Rom. 5:8).

Ad Limina **Address, Rome, 1993**

↜

. . . The sense of sin disappears when—as can happen in the education of youth, in the mass media, and even in education within the family—it is wrongly identified with a morbid feeling of guilt, or with the mere transgression of legal norms and precepts. The loss of the sense of sin is thus a form or consequence of the *denial of God*: not only in the form of atheism but also in the form of secularism. If sin is the breaking off of one's filial relationship to God in order to situate one's life outside of obedience to him, then to sin is not merely to deny God. To sin is also to live as if he did not exist, to eliminate him from one's daily life.

Reconciliatio et Paenitentia, **18**

🔊

Sin, in the proper sense, is always a *personal act,* since it is an act of freedom on the part of an individual person, and not properly of a group or community. This individual may be conditioned, incited, and influenced by numerous and powerful external factors. He may also be subjected to tendencies, defects, and habits linked with his personal condition. In not a few cases such external and internal factors may attenuate, to a greater or lesser degree, the person's freedom and therefore his responsibility and guilt. But it is a truth of faith, also confirmed by our experience and reason, that the human person is free. This truth cannot be disregarded, in order to place the blame for individuals' sins on external factors such as structures, systems, or other people.

Reconciliatio et Paenitentia, **16**

🔊

The Lord's question, "What have you done?" which Cain cannot escape, is addressed also to the people of today, to make them realize the extent and gravity of the attacks against life which continue to mark human history; to make them discover what causes these attacks and feeds them; and to make them ponder seriously the consequences which derive from these attacks for the existence of individuals and peoples. Some threats come from nature itself, but they are made worse by the culpable indifference and negligence of those who could in some cases remedy them. Others are the result of situations of violence, hatred, and conflicting interests, which lead people to attack others through murder, war, slaughter, and genocide.

Evangelium Vitae, 10

☙

No one wishing to investigate the mystery of sin can ignore [the] link between cause and effect. As a rupture with God, sin is an act of disobedience by a creature who rejects, at least implicitly, the very one from whom he came and who sustains him in life. It is therefore a suicidal act. Since by sinning man refuses to submit to God, his internal balance is also destroyed and it is precisely within himself that contradictions and conflicts arise. Wounded in this way, man almost inevitably causes damage to the fabric of his relationship with others and with the created world.

Reconciliatio et Paenitentia, 15

☙

"Forgiveness" is a word spoken by the lips of a man to whom some evil has been done. It is, in fact, the word of the human heart. In this word of the heart each of us endeavors to go beyond the frontier of hostility, which can separate us from the other; he tries to reconstruct the interior space of understanding, contact, bond.

Address, Rome, 1981

ॐ

With humanity's wounding by sin, our internal unity has been sundered. Estranging itself from God's friendship, man's heart has become a place of torment and conflict, a veritable battleground. Tortured and divided within himself, man is estranged from his neighbors. It is not in God's original plan, however, for man to be an enemy to man—*homo hominis lupus*. Man was intended to be brother to man. God's design reveals a dialectic not of confrontation, but of love that makes all things new, a love flowing from the spiritual rock that is Christ.

Homily, "Peace and Reconciliation," 2

ॐ

To speak of reconciliation and Penance is, for the men and women of our time, an invitation to rediscover, translated into their own way of speaking, the very words with which our Savior and Teacher Jesus Christ began his preaching: "Repent, and believe in the Gospel," that is to say, accept the good news of love, of adoption as children of God and hence of brotherhood.

Reconciliatio et Paenitentia, 1

ॐ

Man prepares the way of the Lord and straightens His paths—when he examines his own conscience; when he searches his works, his words, his thoughts; when he calls good and evil by their names; when he does not hesitate to confess his sins in the Sacrament of Penance, repenting and resolving not to sin again.

Insegnamenti V, 3, 1620–23

ॐ

As a personal act, sin has its first and most important consequences in the *sinner himself*: that is, in his relationship with God, who is the very foundation of human life; and also in his spirit, weakening his will and clouding his intellect.

Reconciliatio et Paenitentia, 16

ॐ

. . . Christ speaks of all moral evil, of all sin, that is, of transgressions of the various commandments, and he enumerates "evil thoughts, murder, adultery, fornication, theft, false witness, slander," without confining Himself to a specific kind of sin. It follows that the concept of "purity" and "impurity" in the moral sense is in the first place a general concept, not a specific one: so that all moral good is a manifestation of purity, and all moral evil is a manifestation of impurity.

Audience, Rome, 1980

෴

Reconciliation becomes necessary because there has been the break of sin from which derive all the other forms of break within man and about him. Reconciliation therefore, in order to be complete, necessarily requires liberation from sin, which is to be rejected in its deepest roots. Thus a close internal link unites *conversion* and *reconciliation*. It is impossible to split these two realities or to speak of one and say nothing of the other.

Reconciliatio et Paenitentia, 4

෴

Christ taught us to forgive. Forgiveness is indispensable also for God to put to human conscience some questions to which He expects an answer in complete interior truth. . . . Christ taught us to forgive. He taught Peter to forgive "seventy times seven times" (Mt. 18:22). God Himself forgives when man answers with the whole interior truth of conversion the question addressed to his conscience and to his heart.

Address, Rome, 1981

෴

Life . . . is a precious good, in its entirety and in every part. Those who spend their energies to defend it, to restore its normal efficiency, to promote its full development, acquire the right to the gratitude of every fellow creature of theirs. On the contrary, those who dare to attack it in any way stain themselves with a serious crime and incur the severe condemnation of that judge against which there is no appeal: conscience, the mirror of God.

Address, Rome, 1981

༄

. . . Christ does not invite man to return to the state of original innocence, because humanity has irrevocably left it behind, but He calls him to rediscover—on the foundation of the perennial, and, so to speak, indestructible meanings of what is "human"— the living forms of the "new man." In this way a link, or rather a continuity, is established between the "beginning" and the perspective of redemption.

Audience, Rome, 1980

༄

SPIRITUALITY

Although each individual has the right to be respected in his own journey in search of the truth, there exists a prior moral obligation, and a grave one at that, and to adhere to it once it is known. As Cardinal John Henry Newman, that outstanding defender of the rights of the conscience, forcefully put it: "Conscience has rights because it has duties."

Splendor Veritatis, 34

Because men are persons, with intellect and freedom setting them apart from all other creatures in the visible world, they cannot see their own lives in any other light. The pilgrimage analogy, the comparison with the road to be traveled, is particularly apt for mankind (cf. Heb. 13,14). *Homo viator.* A pilgrim on his way to the absolute (cf. *Lumen Gentium*, n. 49–50). These and similar expressions bear out the eschatological character of the human being in the religious sense too. Man reaches out towards God, his final destination. He travels towards the holy city (cf.

Ps. 122 [121], 1–4; Is. 2:2–5; 35:10), the sanctuary which is accessible to him alone. The dimension of the "sacrum," the "sacral" values: these constitute the highest and most definitive spheres of human life and the sphere of man's most complete self-fulfillment. In this dimension man becomes more fully himself. Through the medium of the "sacrum" the whole of the human life is sublimated, raised to "above"; its natural tendency to remain "below" is thus countered (cf. Jn. 3:3–7; 8:23; Col. 3:1–2; Jas. 1:17; 3:15–17). By contemplating the sacral values and adopting them as his own, man progresses in self-affirmation and self-fulfillment.

Sign of Contradiction, **18.1**

ॐ

When a person is entirely open to the breath of God's love, he becomes caught up in a spiritual "adventure" far beyond anything imaginable.

Homily, Rome, 1993

ॐ

The eclipse of the sense of God and of man inevitably leads to a practical materialism, which breeds individualism, utilitarianism, and hedonism. Here too we see the permanent validity of the apostle: "And since they did not see fit to acknowledge God, God gave them up to a base mind and to improper conduct"

(Rom. 1:28). The values of being are replaced by those of having. The only goal which counts is the pursuit of one's own material well-being. The so-called "quality of life" primarily or exclusively as economic efficiency, inordinate consumerism, physical beauty and pleasure, to the neglect of the more profound dimensions—interpersonal, spiritual, and religious—of existence.

Evangelium Vitae, 23

೫

There are . . . false prophets and false teachers of how to live. First of all there are those who teach people to leave the body, time, and space in order to be able to enter into what they call "true life." They condemn creation, and in the name of deceptive spirituality they lead thousands of young along the paths of an impossible liberation which eventually leaves them even more isolated, victims of their own lives. . . . Seemingly at the opposite extreme, there are the teachers of the "fleeting moment," who invite people to give free rein to every instinctive urge or longing, with the result that individuals fall prey to a sense of anguish and anxiety, leading them to seek refuge in false, artificial paradises, such as that of drugs. . . . There are also those who teach that the meaning of life lies solely in the quest for success, that accumulation of wealth, the development of personal abilities, without regard for the needs of others or respect for values, at times not even for the fundamental value of life itself.

Address, Rome, 1992

꒚

The vocation in which one discovers in depth the evangelical law of giving, a law inscribed in human nature, is itself a gift! It is a gift overflowing with the deepest content of the Gospel, a gift which reflects the divine and human image of the mystery of the Redemption of the world.

Redemptionis Donum, 13

꒚

America, throw open your doors to Christ! Let the seed planted five centuries ago make all areas of your life fruitful: individuals and families, culture and work, economics and politics, the present and future.

Homily, Santo Domingo, 1992

꒚

My dear friends, what is holiness if not the joyful experience of the love of God and the encounter with him in prayer? Being holy means living in profound communication with the God of joy, having a heart free from sin and from the sadness of the world.

Address, Rome, 1995

꒚

We cannot live without hope. We have to have some purpose in life, some meaning to our existence. We have to aspire to something. Without hope, we begin to die. Why does it sometimes happen that a seemingly healthy person, successful in the eyes of the world, takes an overdose of sleeping pills and commits suicide? Why, on the other hand, do we see a seriously disabled person with a great zest for life? Is it not because of hope? The one has lost all hope; in the other, hope is alive and overflowing. Clearly then, hope does not stem from talents and gifts, or from physical health and success! It comes from something else. To be more precise, hope comes from someone else, someone beyond ourselves.

Address, Los Angeles, 1987

༅

The work of moral reconstruction needs a generous investment of energies in the field of spiritual values, which have priority over all material values, as important as they may be.

Audience, Rome, 1992

༅

The present-day phenomenon of secularism is truly serious not simply as regards the individual, but in some ways as regards whole communities, as the council has already indicated: "Growing numbers of people are abandoning religion in practice." At other times I myself have recalled the phenomenon of de-Christianization which strikes long-standing Christian people and which continually calls for re-evangelization.

Human longing and the need for religion, however, are not able to be totally extinguished. When persons in conscience have the courage to face the more serious questions of human existence—particularly questions related to the purpose of life, to suffering and to dying—they are unable to make their own words of truth uttered by St. Augustine: "You have made us to yourself, O Lord, and our hearts are restless until they rest in you." In the same manner the present-day world bears witness to this as well, in ever-increasing and impressive ways, through an openness to a spiritual and transcendent outlook towards life; the renewed interest in religious research; a return to the sense of the sacred and to prayer; and the demand for freedom to call upon the name of the Lord.

Christifideles Laici, 4

༄

Just as it is difficult to live and to give witness of evangelical poverty in a society of consumerism and affluence, it is also difficult to be recognized as religious, in the Absolute of God, in an age of secularization. The tendency toward leveling out, when it does not invert values, seems to favor anonymity of people; to be as most are; to go unnoticed. It is rather the characteristic of being "salt" and "light" (Mt. 5:13 ff.) in the world that carries on Christ's call, especially for those who are consecrated to Him. Likewise there remains in force the promise: "Whoever then will acknowledge me before men, I will acknowledge him before my Father in heaven" (Mt. 10:32).

Address, Fátima, 1982

࿇

Given the prevailing view that happiness consists in satisfying oneself and being satisfied with oneself, the Church must proclaim even more vigorously that it is only God's grace, not therapeutic or self-convincing schemes, which can heal the divisions in the human heart caused by sinfulness (cf. Rom. 3:24; Eph. 2:5).

Ad Limina **Address, 1993**

࿇

. . . If one wants human thought to harvest its ripest fruits, especially in the search for metaphysical truths, it is necessary to cultivate an ethic of thought, one which is not limited to striving for logical correctness, but which situates the mind's activity in a spiritual atmosphere rich in humility, sincerity, courage, honesty, trust, concern for others, openness to the mystery. This all-encompassing ethic of "thinking" does not excuse one from searching but rather facilitates and supports it, and even gives it direction in matters concerning the mystery, because of the intrinsic connection between the *verum* [truth] and the *bonum* [good], which in God coincides with His very essence.

Address, University of Vilnius, 1993

༈

It cannot be denied that, for many Christians, the spiritual life is passing through a time of uncertainty which affects not only their moral life but also their life of prayer and the theological correctness of their faith. Faith, already put to the test by the challenges of our times. It is sometimes disoriented by erroneous theological views, the spread of which is abetted by the crisis of obedience vis-à-vis the Church's magisterium.

Tertio Millennio Adveniente, 36

༈

From the moment of the very first denial, Truth—the divine Truth—will always seek, in ways known only to itself, to penetrate world history, to enter the hearts and minds of men. The father of lies will never cease to deny it. But the one who said of himself: "I am the way and the truth . . ." (Jn. 14:6) is certain of victory. The great heart that opened in the first chapters of Genesis does not withdraw and close again when faced with the lie, but sheds over the whole of human history, in every age including our own, the light of boundless hope.

Sign of Contradiction, 6.1

༈

Elevation of the soul is accomplished through knowledge of the Lord and His ways. "Your ways, O Lord, make known to me; teach me your paths, guide me in your truth and teach me. . . ." (Ps. 25:4–5)

As you see, it is not a matter of abstract knowledge but of knowledge having influence upon life. "Teach me your paths" means teach me to live in conformity with God's will.

Insegnamenti V, 3, 1465–72

✧

Happiness springs from the knowledge of truth, from the vision of God face to face, from sharing in His life. This happiness is so profoundly a part of man's deepest aspiration that the words just cited above from the First Letter to Timothy seem fully justified: the One who has created man with this fundamental desire cannot behave differently from what the revealed text indicates; He cannot but want "everyone to be saved and to come to knowledge of the truth."

Crossing the Threshold of Hope

✧

Faithful to the truth, brothers and sisters, we continue to share in the kingship of Christ, serving as He, the Lord and Master, did and taught. This is the path: Christians in the warmth of personal privacy; Christians within the household, as spouses, fathers, and mothers and children of our families, in the "domestic Church"; Christians in the street, as men and women located there; Christians in community life, at work, in our professional and managerial meetings, in groups, in unions, in pleasure, during our free time, etc.; Christians in society, both those who have elevated positions or those who serve humbly; Christians in social and political participation, and finally, always Christians, in the presence and glorification of God, Lord of life and of history.

Address, Lisbon, Portugal, 1982

جر

The exhilarating adventure of human thought lies in [the] essential dynamic that situates man between his awareness of limits and the need for the absolute. For this reason, when man "thinks" deeply, with intellectual rigor and integrity of heart, he is on the way towards a possible encounter with God.

Address, University of Vilnius, 1993

جر

What can I wish for you but that you will always listen to these words of Mary, the Mother of Christ: "Do whatever he tells you." And may you accept these words with your hearts, because they were uttered from the heart. From the heart of Mother. And that you will fulfill them: "God has chosen you . . . calling you to this/with our Gospel, for possession of the glory of our Lord/Jesus Christ."

Insegnamenti VIII, **1**, 164–65

ॐ

The eyes of faith behold a wonderful scene: that of a countless number of lay people, both women and men, busy at work in their daily life and activity, oftentimes far from view and quite unacclaimed by the world, unknown to the world's great personages but nonetheless looked upon in love by the Father, untiring laborers who work in the Lord's vineyard. Confident and steadfast through the power of God's grace, these are the humble yet great builders of the Kingdom of God in history.

Christifideles Laici, 17

ॐ

This new life which Christ has given us becomes our spiritual life, our interior life. We therefore discover within ourselves the interior person with its qualities, talents, worthy desires and ideals; but we also discover our weaknesses, our vices, our evil inclinations: Selfishness, pride, and sensuality. We perfectly understand how much the first of these aspects of our humanity needs to be developed and strengthened, and how much instead the second one must be overcome, combated and transformed. In this way—in living contact with Jesus, in the contact of the disciple with the Master—there begins and develops the most sublime activity of man: Work on himself that aims at the formation of his own humanity.

Homily, Jasna Gora, Poland, 1979

જ

Your spirituality must draw from the spring that is Christ, the Teacher of teachers, Pastor of our souls, the supreme Model of all educators and of all education.

Address, Rio Grande do Sul, Brazil, 1980

જ

THE STATE

Authentic democracy is possible only in a state ruled by law, and on the basis of a correct conception of the human person. It requires that the necessary conditions be present for the advancement both of the individual through education and formation in true ideals, and of the "subjectivity" of society through the creation of structures of participation and shared responsibility. Nowadays there is a tendency to claim that agnosticism and skeptical relativism are the philosophy and the basic attitude which correspond to democratic forms of political life. Those who are convinced that they know the truth and firmly adhere to it are considered unreliable from a democratic point of view, since they do not accept that truth is determined by the majority, or that it is subject to variation according to different political trends. It must be observed in this regard that if there is no ultimate truth to guide and direct political activity, then ideas and convictions can easily be manipulated for reasons of power. As history demonstrates, a democracy without values easily turns into open or thinly disguised total-itarianism.

Centessimus Annus, 46

༄

The history of a nation ought to be appraised according to its contribution to the progress of man, of his awareness, compassion, and conscience, as these faculties are the foundation, the essence, and the source of the power of culture.

Address, Warsaw, 1979

༄

The state cannot limit itself to "favoring one portion of the citizens," namely the rich and prosperous, nor can it "neglect the other," which clearly represents the majority of society. Otherwise, there would be a violation of that law of justice which ordains that every person should receive his due.

Centessimus Annus, 10

༄

The original and inalienable right to life is questioned or denied on the basis of a parliamentary vote or the will of one part of the people—even if it is the majority. This is the sinister result of a relativism which reigns unopposed: The "right" ceases to be such, because it is no longer firmly founded on the inviolable dignity of the person, but is made subject to the will of the stronger part. In this way democracy, contradicting its own principles, effectively moves toward a form of totalitarianism. The state is no longer the "common home" where all can live together on the basis of principles of fundamental equality, but is transformed into a tyrant state which arrogates to itself the right to dispose of the life of the weakest and most defenseless members, from the unborn child to the elderly, in the name of a public interest which is really nothing but the interest of one part.

Evangelium Vitae, **20**

⨍

The weakness of Christians brings into even greater relief the power of Christ. Without Christ it is not possible to resolve issues which are daily becoming more complicated for the international institutions and organizations, as well as for the various governments involved in the conflict.

Address, Rome, 1994

⨍

Every political power, in effect, has meaning and justification only in the search for the common good of all. This power finds its limitation in the acceptance of international conventions and in respect for the fundamental rights of individuals, which no one should be able to violate and which are guaranteed by the human conscience and, for believers, by the Author of that conscience, the Creator of mankind.

Address, Queluz, Portugal, 1982

ꙮ

Another task of the State is that of overseeing and directing the exercise of human rights in the economic sector. However, primary responsibility in this area belongs not to the State but to individuals and to the various groups and associations which make up society. The State could not directly ensure the right to work for all its citizens unless it controlled every aspect of economic life and restricted the free initiative of individuals. This does not mean, however, that the State has no competence in this domain, as was claimed by those who argued against any rules in the economic sphere. Rather, the State has a duty to sustain business activities by creating conditions which will ensure job opportunities where they are lacking or by supporting them in moments of crisis. . . . In addition to the tasks of harmonizing and guiding development, in exceptional circumstances the State can also exercise a *substitute function*, when social sectors or business systems are too weak or are just getting under way, and are not equal to the task at hand. Such supplementary interventions, which are justified by urgent reasons touching the common good, must be as brief as possible, so as to avoid removing permanently from society and business systems the functions which are properly theirs, and so as to avoid enlarging excessively the sphere of state intervention to the detriment of both economic and civil freedom.

Centessimus Annus, **48**

꒜

Human-Christian values triumph when any system is reformed that authorizes the exploitation of any human being; when upright service and honesty in public servants is promoted; when the dispensing of justice is fair and the same for all; when responsible use is made of the material and energy resources of the world—resources that are meant for the benefit of all; when the environment is preserved intact for the future generation. Human-Christian values triumph by subjecting political and economic considerations to human dignity, by making them serve the cause of man—every person created by God, every brother and sister redeemed by Christ.

Address, Philadelphia, 1979

꒜

The risk in democratic regimes is to become a system of rules insufficiently rooted in those values that are undeniable because they are grounded in the essential nature of man, which must be the basis of all social life and which no majority can deny, without ruinous consequences for the individual and for society. The Church has vigorously raised her voice against this corruption of freedom, in both the political and economic spheres.

Address, University of Vilnius, 1993

༜

. . . Every person has a right and duty to participate in public life, albeit in a diversity and complementarity of forms, levels, tasks, and responsibilites. Charges of careerism, idolatry of power, egoism, and corruption that are oftentimes directed at persons in government, parliaments, the ruling classes, or political parties, as well as the common opinion that participating in politics is an absolute moral danger, does not in the least justify either skepticism or an absence on the part of Christians in public life.

Christifideles Laici, **42**

༜

The painful experience of the history of my own country, Poland, has shown me how important national sovereignty is when it is served by a state worthy of the name and free in its decisions; how important it is for the protection not only of a people's legitimate material interests but also of its culture and its soul.

Address to the Organization of American States, 1979

༜

The individual today is often suffocated between two poles represented by the State and the marketplace. At times it seems as though he exists only as a producer and consumer of goods, or as an object of state administration. People lose sight of the fact that life in society has neither the market nor the State as its final purpose, since life itself has a unique value which the State and the market must serve. Man remains above all a being who seeks the truth and strives to live in that truth, deepening the understanding of it through a dialogue which involves past and future generations.

Centessimus Annus, 49

৵

. . . Development must not be understood solely in economic terms, but in a way that is fully human. It is not only a question of raising all peoples to the level currently enjoyed by the richest countries, but rather of building up a more decent life through united labor, of concretely enhancing every individual's dignity and creativity, as well as his capacity to respond to his personal vocation, and thus to God's call. The apex of development is the exercise of the right and duty to seek God, to know him and to live in accordance with that knowledge. In the totalitarian and authoritarian regimes, the principle that force predominates over reason was carried to the extreme. A person was compelled to submit to a conception of reality imposed on him by coercion, and not reached by virtue of his own reason and the exercise of his own freedom. This principle must be overturned and total recognition must be given to *the rights of the human conscience*, which is bound only to the truth, both natural and revealed. The recognition of these rights represents the primary foundation of every authentically free political order.

Centessimus Annus, 29

⤳

Public life on behalf of the person and society finds its *basic standard* in *the pursuit of the common good*, as the good of *everyone* and as the good of each person taken as a *whole*, which is guaranteed and offered in a fitting manner to people both as individuals and in groups for their free and responsible acceptance.

Christifideles Laici, 42

⤳

. . . The social nature of man is not completely fulfilled in the State, but is realized in various intermediary groups, beginning with the family and including economic, social, political, and cultural groups which stem from human nature itself and have their own autonomy, always with a view to the common good.

Centessimus Annus, 13

⤳

Public life on behalf of the person and society finds its basic *standard* in *the pursuit of the common good*, as the good of *everyone* and as the good of each person taken as a *whole*, which is guaranteed and offered in a fitting manner to people both as individuals and in groups for their free and responsible acceptance. . . . Furthermore, public life on behalf of the person and society finds its *continuous line of action* in *the defense and the promotion of justice* understood to be a "virtue," an understanding which requires education as well as a moral "force" that sustains the obligation to foster the rights and duties of each and everyone based on the personal dignity of each human being.

Christifideles Laici, 42

༺

STEWARDSHIP

We are all citizens of the earth. Our work is of extraordinary importance for the achievement of the common good. But we are also citizens of the kingdom of God, which is not of the world and which comes to us as a divine gift and as a Christian vocation.

Address, Vila Vicosa, Portugal, 1982

࿓

The earth is man's because God has entrusted it to man. . . . The earth is a gift of God, a gift that he makes to all human beings, men and women, whom he wishes to see joined together in a single family, and relating to one another in a fraternal spirit.

Homily, Recife, Brazil, 1980

࿓

In addition to the irrational destruction of the natural environment, we must also mention the more serious destruction of the *human environment*, something which is by no means receiving the attention it deserves. Although people are rightly worried—though much less than they should be—about preserving the natural habitats of the various animal species threatened with extinction, because they realize that each of these species makes its particular contribution to the balance of nature in general, too little effort is made to *safeguard the moral conditions for an authentic "human ecology."*

Centessimus Annus, 38

꒐

. . . The land must be conserved with care since it is intended to be fruitful for generation upon generation. You who live in the heartland of America have been entrusted with some of the earth's best land: the soil so rich in minerals, the climate so favorable for producing bountiful crops, with fresh water and unpolluted air available all around you. You are stewards of some of the most important resources God has given to the world. Therefore conserve the land well, so that your children and your children's children and generations after them will inherit an even richer land than was entrusted to you. But also remember what the heart of your vocation is. While it is true here that farming today provides an economic livelihood for the farmer, still it will always be more than an enterprise of profit-making. In farming, you cooperate with the Creator in the very sustenance of life on earth.

Address, Des Moines, 1979

꒐

Man dominates the earth by the very fact of domesticating animals, rearing them and obtaining from them the food and clothing he needs, and by the fact of being able to extract various natural resources from the earth and the seas. But man "subdues the earth" much more when he begins to cultivate it and then to transform its products, adapting them to his own use.

Laborem Exercens, 5

༈

Man's knowledge of the world is a way of sharing in the Creator's knowledge. It constitutes, therefore, a first degree of man's resemblance with God, an act of respect towards him; for everything that we discover pays homage to the First Truth.

Insegnamenti II, 1, 748

༈

Not only has God given the earth to humanity, which must use it with respect for the original good purpose for which it was given, but man too is God's gift to man. A person must therefore respect the natural and moral structure with which he has been endowed. In this context, mention should be made of the serious problems of modern urbanization, of the need for urban planning which is concerned with how people are to live, and of the attention which should be given to a "social ecology" of work.

Centessimus Annus, 38

༈

. . . According to the original designs of God, man is called to become lord of the earth, "to master it" (Gen. 1:28) by the superiority of his intelligence and the activity of his arms. He is the center of creation.

Address, Porto, Portugal, 1982

න

We must see another's poverty as our own and be convinced that the poor can wait no longer.

Homily, Santo Domingo, 1992

න

Man has to subdue the earth and dominate it, because as "the image of God" he is a person, that is to say, a subjective being capable of acting in a planned and rational way, capable of deciding about himself, and with a tendency to self-realization. *As a person, man is therefore the subject of work.*

Laborem Exercens, 6

න

Solutions must be sought on the global level by establishing a true economy of communion and sharing of goods, in both the national and international order.

Address, Santo Domingo, 1992

න

Man is a person, man and woman equally so, since both were created in the image and likeness of the personal God. What makes man like God is the fact that—unlike the whole world of other living creatures, including those endowed with senses (*animalia*)—man is also a rational being (*animal rationale*). Thanks to this property, man and woman are able to "dominate" the other creatures of the visible world.

Mulieris Dignitatem, 6

꙳

The first fundamental means to dominate the earth lies in man himself. Man can dominate the earth because he alone—and no other of the living beings—is capable of "tilling it" and transforming it according to his own needs.

Address, Rome, 1979

꙳

The continuing existence of millions of people who suffer hunger or malnutrition and the growing realization that the natural resources are limited make clear that humanity forms a single whole. Pollution of air and water threatens more and more the delicate balance of the biosphere on which present and future generations depend and makes us realize that we all share a common ecological environment. Instant communication has linked finance and trade in worldwide dependence.

Address, Detroit, 1987

꙳

The savant will not . . . treat nature like a slave; but taking his inspiration from Saint Francis of Assisi's "Canticle of Creatures" he will consider it rather as a sister, called to cooperate with him in opening new paths of progress for humanity.

Insegnamenti II, 1, 748

༄

Certain social and cultural manifestations arising in the defense of mankind and the environment, and which must be illuminated with the light of faith, provide examples of the inculturation of the Gospel. This is the case of the environmental movement promoting due respect for nature and against the disordered exploitation of natural resources, with its consequent deterioration in the quality of life. The conviction that "God destined the earth and all it contains for all men and all peoples" (*Gaudium et Spes*, n. 69) must inspire a system of resource-management that is more just and better coordinated on the global level. The Church makes concern for the environment her own and urges governments to protect this heritage according to the criteria of the common good.

Address, Santo Domingo, 1992

༄

WOMEN

I wish to express the deep gratitude of the Church for *all the contributions made by women* over the centuries to the life of the Church and of society. In speaking of the role of women, special mention must of course be made of their contribution, in partnership with their husbands, in begetting life and in educating their children. . . . The Church is convinced, however, that all the special gifts of women are needed in an ever increasing measure in her life, and for this reason hopes for their fuller participation in her activities. Precisely because of their equal dignity and responsibility, the access of women to public functions must be ensured. Regardless of the role they perform, the Church proclaims the dignity of women as women—a dignity equal to men's dignity, and revealed as such in the account of creation contained in the word of God.

Address, San Francisco, 1987

In dealing with *the specific rights of women as women*, it is necessary to return again and again to the immutable basis of Christian anthropology as it is foreshadowed in the scriptural account of the creation of man—as male and female—in the image and likeness of God. Both man and woman are created in the image of *the personhood of God*, with inalienable personal dignity, and in complementarity one with the other. Whatever violates the complementarity of women and men, whatever impedes the true communion of persons according to the complementarity of sexes offends the dignity of both women and men.

Ad Limina **Address, 1988**

ॐ

We especially thank consecrated women. Their total giving of themselves to Christ, their life of adoration and of intercession for the world, bear witness to the Church's holiness. Their service to God's people and to society in various fields of evangelizing—pastoral activity, education, care of the sick, the poor, and the abandoned—make visible the motherly face of the Church.

Address, Rome, 1994

ॐ

. . . Women have the task of *assuring the moral dimension of culture*, the dimension of culture, the dimension—namely of *a culture worthy of the person*—of an individual yet social life.

Christifideles Laici, 51

꒜

. . . Woman has an understanding, sensitive and compassionate heart that allows her to give a delicate, concrete style to charity.

Address, Rome, 1994

꒜

In our times the question of "women's rights" has taken on new significance in the broad context of the rights of the human person. The biblical and evangelical message sheds light on this cause which is the object of much attention today, by safeguarding the truth about the "unity" of the "two," that is to say the truth about that dignity and vocation that result from the specific diversity and personal originality of man and woman. . . . In the name of liberation from male "domination," women must not appropriate to themselves male characteristics contrary to their own feminine "originality." There is a well-founded fear that if they take this path, women will not "reach fulfillment," but instead will deform and lose what constitutes their essential richness. It is indeed an enormous richness.

Mulieris Dignitatem, 10

꒜

May [women] be witnesses, messengers, and teachers of peace in relations between generations, in the family, in the cultural, social, and political life of nations, and particularly in situations of conflict and war. May they continue to follow the path which leads to peace, a path which many courageous and far-sighted women have walked before them.

Address, Rome, 1994

༈

Care must be taken that woman is not, for financial reasons, necessarily tied down to work that is too heavy and hours of work that are too long, in addition to all her responsibilities as homemaker and educator of her children. Society . . . should make every effort to organize itself differently.

Sermon, Fifteenth International Congress of the Family, 1980

༈

If anyone has the task of advancing the dignity of women in the Church and society, it is women themselves who must recognize their responsibility as leading characters. There is still much effort to be done in many parts of the world and in various surroundings to destroy that unjust and deleterious mentality which considers the human being as a thing, as an object to buy and sell, as an instrument for selfish interests or for pleasure only. Women themselves, for the most part, are the prime victims of such a mentality. Only through openly acknowledging the personal dignity of women is the first step taken to promote the full participation of women in Church life as well as in social and public life.

Christifideles Laici, 49

꙳

Sadly, a long history of sin has disturbed and continues to disturb God's original plan for the couple, for the male and the female, thus standing in the way of its complete fulfillment. We need to return to this plan, to proclaim it forcefully, so that women in particular—who have suffered more from its failure to be fulfilled—can finally give full expression to their womanhood and their dignity.

Address, Rome, 1994

꙳

. . . Each man must look within himself to see whether she who was entrusted to him as a sister in humanity, as a spouse, has not become in his heart an object of adultery; to see whether she who, in different ways, is the cosubject of existence in the world, has not become for him an "object": an object of pleasure, of exploitation.

Mulieris Dignitatem, 14

꙳

If our century has been characterized in liberal societies by a growing *feminism,* it might be said that this trend is a reaction to the lack of respect accorded each woman. . . . I think that a certain contemporary feminism finds its roots in the absence of true respect for woman. Revealed truth teaches us something different. Respect for woman, amazement at the mystery of womanhood, and finally the nuptial love of God Himself and of Christ, as expressed in the Redemption, are all elements that have never been completely absent in the faith and life of the Church. This can be seen in a rich tradition of customs and practices that, regrettably, is nowadays being eroded. In our civilization woman has become, before all else, an object of pleasure. . . . It is very significant, on the other hand, that in the midst of this very situation the authentic theology of woman is being reborn. The spiritual beauty, the particular genius, of women is being rediscovered. The bases for the consolidation of the position of women in life, not family life but also social and cultural life, are being redefined.

Crossing the Threshold of Hope

ॐ

The moral and spiritual strength of a woman is joined to her awareness that God entrusts the human being to her in a special way. Of course, God entrusts every human being to each and every other human being. But this entrusting concerns women in a special way—precisely by reason of their femininity—and this in a particular way determines their vocation.

Mulieris Dignitatem, 30

჻

The work of building peace can hardly overlook the need to acknowledge and promote the dignity of women as persons, called to play a unique role in educating for peace.

Address, Rome, 1994

჻

. . . The Christian message about the dignity of women is contradicted by that persistent mentality which considers the human being not as a person but as a thing, as an object of trade, at the service of selfish interest and mere pleasure: the first victims of this mentality are women. . . . This mentality produces very bitter fruits, such as contempt for men and for women, slavery, oppression of the weak, pornography, prostitution—especially in an organized form—and all those various forms of discrimination that exist in the fields of education, employment, wages, etc. . . . Besides, many forms of degrading discrimination still persist today in a great part of our society that affect and seriously harm particular categories of women, as for example childless wives, widows, separated or divorced women, and unmarried mothers.

Familiaris Consortio, **24**

⨯

The true advancement of women requires that labor should be structured in such a way that women do not have to pay for their advancement by abandoning what is specific to them and at the expense of the family, in which women as mothers have an irreplaceable role.

Laborem Exercens, **19**

⨯

When we say that the woman is the one who receives love in order to love in return, this refers not only or above all to the specific spousal relationship of marriage. It means something more universal, based on the very fact of her being a woman within all the interpersonal relationships which, in the most varied ways, shape society and structure the interaction between all persons—men and women. In this broad and diversified context, a woman represents a particular value by the fact that she is a human person, and at the same time this particular person, by the fact of her femininity. This concerns each and every woman, independently of the cultural context in which she lives, and independently of her spiritual, psychological, and physical characteristics, as for example, age, education, health, work, and whether she is married or single.

Mulieris Dignitatem, 29

꒷

When women are able fully to share their gifts with the whole community, the very way in which society understands and organizes itself is improved, and comes to reflect in a better way the substantial unity of the human family. Here we see the most important condition for the consolidation of authentic peace. The growing presence of women in social, economic, and political life at the local, national, and international levels is thus a very positive development. Women have a full right to become actively involved in all areas of public life, and this right must be affirmed and guaranteed, also, where necessary, through appropriate legislation.

Address, Rome, 1994

꒷

There is no doubt that the equal dignity and responsibility of men and women fully justifies women's access to public functions. On the other hand the true advancement of women requires that clear recognition be given to the value of their maternal and family role, by comparison with all other public roles and all other professions. Furthermore, these roles and professions should be harmoniously combined, if we wish the evolution of society and culture to be truly and fully human. . . . While it must be recognized that women have the same right as men to perform various public functions, society must be structured in such a way that wives and mothers are not in practice compelled to work outside the home, and that their families can live and prosper in a dignified way even when they themselves devote their full time to their own family.

Familiaris Consortio, 23

ↄ

The condition that will assure the rightful presence of woman in the Church and in society is a more penetrating and accurate consideration of the *anthropological foundation for masculinity and femininity* with the intent of clarifying woman's personal identity in relation to man, that is, a diversity yet mutual complementarity, not only as it concerns roles to be held and functions to be performed, but also, and more deeply, as it concerns her makeup and meaning as a person.

Christifideles Laici, 50

ↄ

There are many other aspects involved in the question of women's equal dignity and responsibility. . . . At the basis of all consideration are two firm principles: *the equal human dignity of women and their true feminine humanity.* On the basis of these two principles, *Familiaris Consortio* has already enunciated much of the Church's attitude toward women, which reflects the "sensitive respect of Jesus toward the women that he called to his following and his friendship" (no. 22). As I have stated . . . women are not called to the priesthood. Although the teaching of the Church on this point is quite clear, it in no way alters the fact that women *are indeed an essential part of the Gospel plan to spread the Good News of the Kingdom.* And the Church is irrevocably committed to this truth.

Address, Los Angeles, 1987

જ

Throughout the whole Church a great prayerful reflection still remains to be made on *the teaching of the Church* about women and about their dignity and vocation. . . . The Church is determined to place her full teaching, with all the power with which divine truth is invested, at the service of the cause of women in the modern world—to help clarify their correlative rights and duties, while defending *their feminine dignity and vocation.* The importance of true Christian feminism is so great that every effort must be made to present the principles on which this cause is based, and according to which it can be effectively defended and promoted for the good of all humanity.

Ad Limina **Address, 1988**

જ

. . . A certain number of women rightly feel the need to be understood better, in their dignity as a person, in their rights, in the value of the tasks which are customarily theirs, in their aspiration to realize fully their feminine vocation within the family, but also in society. Some are weary and almost crushed by so many worries and burdens, without finding sufficient understanding and aid. *Some suffer and regret being relegated to tasks which they are told are secondary ones. Some are tempted to seek a solution in movements which claim to "liberate" them, although it would be necessary to ask what liberation it is a question of, and not to mean by the word emancipation from what is their specific vocation as mothers and wives, or imitation, leading to uniformity, of the way in which the male partner finds fulfillment.* And yet all this evolution and turmoil show clearly that there is a real feminine advancement to be pursued, in many respects. The family of course, but also the whole of society and ecclesial communities, need the specific contributions of women.

Address, Fifth International Congress of the Family, 1980

꙳

"God created man in his own image, in the image of God he created him; male and female he created them" (Gen. 1:27). This concise passage contains the fundamental anthropological truths: Man is the high point of the whole order of creation in the visible world; the human race, which takes its origin from the calling into existence of man and woman, crowns the whole work of creation; *both man and woman are human beings to an equal degree*, both are created *in God's image*. This image and likeness of God, which is essential for the human being, is passed on by the man and woman, as spouses and parents, to their descendants . . .

Mulieris Dignitatem, 6

༄

In our day women have made great strides . . . attaining a remarkable degree of self-expression in cultural, social, economic, and political life, as well as, of course, in family life. The journey has been a difficult and complicated one and, at times, not without its share of mistakes. But it has been substantially a positive one, even if it is still unfinished, due to the many obstacles which, in various parts of the world, still prevent women from being acknowledged, respected, and appreciated for their own special dignity.

Address, Rome, 1994

༄

Believers ought to feel the urgency of the call to defend the equal human dignity of all persons, created by God, male and female. The differences between women and men must never be used to oppress or discriminate against the one, or to claim a superior position for the other. Yet we are sadly aware that, in practice, women experience widespread forms of discrimination. There is ample room therefore for believers to work together in order to defend and promote the proper place of women in society as intended by God.

Address, Rome, 1992

༄

. . . The woman has a right to the honor and joy of motherhood as a gift from God and in due course the children also have the right to the care and concern of those who have begotten them, their mothers in particular.

Address, Rome, 1994

༄

WORLD RELIGIONS

Traditional religions have in the past formed one piece with the cultures of the people who practiced them. Among these peoples the same word was often used for religion, custom, and culture. These forces and values held their societies together.

The meeting with Christianity, other religions, and also with Western culture, and especially with modern science and technology and urbanization, has affected these societies and their traditional religions. Nevertheless the influence of traditional religion remains strong, particularly at moments of crisis.

Letter, Pontifical Council for Interreligious Dialogue, 1993

ッ

In our century in particular, events have taken place that clash profoundly with the truth of the Gospel. I allude above all to the *two World Wars* and to the concentration and extermination camps. Paradoxically, these events may have reinforced ecumenical consciousness among divided Christians. In this regard, the *extermination of the Jews* certainly had a special role. It placed before both the Church and Christianity the issue of the relationship between the Old and New Testaments.

Crossing the Threshold of Hope

ॐ

. . . We also join with so many Christians who, all over the world, despite our divisions, join with Christ in asking for the great grace of that unity which he so ardently desired, and which his power alone can bring about. . . . The fact that Christians pray together in this way is already in itself a grace and a guarantee of future graces.

Insegnamenti VII, 214

ॐ

Of course, we unfortunately have to acknowledge the fact that the millennium which is about to end is the one in which there have occurred the great separations between Christians. All believers in Christ, therefore, following the example of the Apostles, must fervently strive to conform their thinking and acting to the will of the Holy Spirit, "the true principle of the Church's unity," so that all who have been baptized in the one Spirit in order to make up one body may be brethren joined in the celebration of the same Eucharist, "a sacrament of love, a sign of unity, a bond of charity."

Dominum et Vivificantem, 62

ॐ

Above all, we must always be more docile to the Holy Spirit, and to how the Spirit speaks to the Churches today. In all things we need—wherever possible—to show our concern for giving testimony together to Christ and to his gospel, in our world of today which offers us such rich possibilities, but which is also afflicted with so many evils that corrupt it and undermine it. Think of hunger, of the drug plague, of jobless youth. Then there are all the fields in which Christians have much to say, where together they can, through common effort, bring about a reaffirmed respect for human persons, for their moral greatness which today is attacked on all fronts, for humanity's continual advance towards liberty, progress, and peace.

Insegnamenti **VIII, 1, 1998**

༄

Unity is not the result of human policies or hidden and mysterious intentions. Instead, unity springs from conversion of the heart, and from sincere acceptance of the unchanging principles laid down by Christ for His Church. Particularly important among these principles is the effective communion of all parts of the Church with her visible foundation: Peter, the Rock.

Message to Chinese Catholics, 1995

༄

Authentic ecumenical dialogue requires of the theologians a great maturity and certainty in the truth professed by the Church; it requires of them a particular fidelity to the teaching of the magisterium. Only by means of such a dialogue can "ecumenism" . . . become an ever more mature reality; in other words, only on the path of a great self-commitment of the Church, inspired by the certitude of faith and by confidence in the power of Christ in which, from the start, the pioneers of this undertaking were distinguished.

Redemptor Hominis, 55

ॐ

We must strive to construct together a present and a future more in line with Christ's will for the unity of all his disciples.

Insegnamenti VIII, 1, 1997

ॐ

Nor must we forget the brethren of other Churches. For the cause of ecumenism is so lofty and such a sensitive issue that we may not keep silent about it. How often do we meditate together on the last wish of Christ who asked the Father for the gift of unity for the disciples. Who does not remember how much St. Paul stressed the "unity of the spirit" from which the followers of Christ might have the same love, being "of one accord, of one Mind?" Therefore one can hardly credit that a deplorable division still exists among Christians. This is a cause of embarrassment and perhaps a scandal to others. And so we wish to proceed along the way that has been so happily opened up, and to encourage whatever can serve to remove the obstacles, since we desire that through common effort full communion may eventually be achieved.

Address, Rome, 1978

. . . The union of Christians cannot be sought in any compromise between the various theological positions, but only in a common encounter in the most ample and mature fullness of Christian truth. This is our desire, and theirs also. It is a duty of mutual honesty.

Insegnamenti **III, 1, 1892**

You are the heirs and keepers of an ancient wisdom. This wisdom in Japan and in the Orient has inspired high degrees of moral life. It has taught you to venerate the pure, transparent, and honest heart. It has inspired you to discover the divine presence in every creature, and especially in every human being.

Address, Tokyo, 1981

The Catholic Church recognizes the truths that are contained in the religious traditions of India. This recognition makes true dialogue possible.

Address, Madras, 1986

&

The religions of the Far East have contributed greatly to the history of morality and culture, forming a national identity in the Chinese, Indians, Japanese, and Tibetans, and also in the peoples of Southeast Asia and the archipelagoes of the Pacific Ocean.

Some of these peoples come from age-old cultures. The indigenous peoples of Australia boast a history tens of thousands of years old, and their ethnic and religious tradition is older than that of Abraham and Moses.

Christ came into the world for all these peoples. He redeemed them all and has His own ways of reaching each of them in the present eschatological phase of salvation history. In fact, in those regions, many accept Him and many more have an implicit faith in Him (cf. Heb. 11:6).

Crossing the Threshold of Hope

&

. . . For thousands of years you have lived in this land and fashioned a culture that endures to this day. And during all this time, the Spirit of God has been with you. Your "Dreaming," which influences your lives so strongly that, no matter what happens, you remain forever people of your culture, is your own way of touching the mystery of God's spirit in you and in creation. You must keep your striving for God and hold on to it in your lives.

You live your lives in spiritual closeness to the land, with its animals, birds, fishes, water-holes, rivers, hills, and mountains. Through your closeness to the land you touched the sacredness of man's relationship with God, for the land was the proof of a power in life greater than yourselves.

The silence of the Bush taught you a quietness of soul that put you in touch with *another world, the world of God's Spirit.*

Address, Australia, 1986

꒰

The Jewish religion is not "extrinsic" to us, but in a certain way is "intrinsic" to our own religion. With Judaism, therefore, we have a relationship which we do not have with any other religion.

Address, Rome, 1986

꒰

Before the vivid memory of the extermination (*Shoah*), it is not permissible for anyone to pass by with indifference. . . . The sufferings endured by the Jews are also for the Catholic Church a motive of sincere sorrow, especially when one thinks of the indifference and sometimes resentment which . . . have divided Jews and Christians.

Address, Rome, 1994

༉

We trust that with the approach of the year 2000, Jerusalem will become the city of peace for the entire world and that all the people will be able to meet there, in particular the believers in the religions that find their birthright in the faith of Abraham.

Interview, *Parade* **magazine, April 3, 1994**

༉

Believers of the great monotheistic religions turn toward the Holy City of Jerusalem, which we know is still today a theater of conflicts and division, but it still remains a sacred patrimony for those who believe in God.

Address, November 1994

༉

. . . The religiosity of Muslims deserves respect. It is impossible not to admire, for example, *their fidelity to prayer.* The image of believers in Allah who, without caring about time and place, fall to their knees and immerse themselves in prayer remains a model for all *those who invoke* the true God, in particular for those Christians who, having deserted their magnificent cathedrals, pray only a little or not at all.

Crossing the Threshold of Hope

ക

Many points common to Muslims and Christians are related to religious piety, such as the importance given to prayer, a regard for morality, and a sense of the dignity of the human person open to the transcendent.

Address, Parakou, Benin, 1994

ക

A separate issue is the *return of ancient gnostic ideas under the guise of the so-called New Age*. We cannot delude ourselves that this will lead toward a renewal of religion. It is only a new way of practicing gnosticism—that attitude of the spirit that, in the name of a profound knowledge of God, results in distorting His Word and replacing it with purely human words. Gnosticism never completely abandoned the realm of Christianity, sometimes taking the shape of a philosophical movement, but more often assuming the characteristics of a religion or parareligion in distinct, if not declared, conflict with all that is essentially Christian.

Crossing the Threshold of Hope

ക